Harvard Business Review

ON

APPRAISING EMPLOYEE PERFORMANCE

D0830202

THE HARVARD BUSINESS REVIEW PAPERBACK SERIES

The series is designed to bring today's managers and professionals the fundamental information they need to stay competitive in a fast-moving world. From the preeminent thinkers whose work has defined an entire field to the rising stars who will redefine the way we think about business, here are the leading minds and landmark ideas that have established the *Harvard Business Review* as required reading for ambitious businesspeople in organizations around the globe.

Other books in the series:

Harvard Business Review Interviews with CEOs

Harvard Business Review on Advances in Strategy

Harvard Business Review on Becoming a High Performance Manager

Harvard Business Review on Brand Management

Harvard Business Review on Breakthrough Leadership

Harvard Business Review on Breakthrough Thinking

Harvard Business Review on Building Personal and Organizational Resilience

Harvard Business Review on Business and the Environment

Harvard Business Review on the Business Value of IT

Harvard Business Review on Change

Harvard Business Review on Compensation

Harvard Business Review on Corporate Ethics

Harvard Business Review on Corporate Governance

Harvard Business Review on Corporate Responsibility

Harvard Business Review on Corporate Strategy

Harvard Business Review on Crisis Management

Harvard Business Review on Culture and Change

Harvard Business Review on Customer Relationship Management

Harvard Business Review on Decision Making

Other books in the series (continued):

Harvard Business Review on Teams That Succeed

Harvard Business Review on Turnarounds

Harvard Business Review on Work and Life Balance

Harvard Business Review

ON

APPRAISING EMPLOYEE PERFORMANCE

A HARVARD BUSINESS REVIEW PAPERBACK

Copyright 2005
Harvard Business School Publishing Corporation
All rights reserved
Printed in the United States of America
12 11 10 09 08   6 5 4 3 2

No part of this publication may be reproduced, stored in or introduced
into a retrieval system, or transmitted, in any form, or by any means
(electronic, mechanical, photocopying, recording, or otherwise),
without the prior permission of the publisher. Requests for permission
should be directed to permissions@harvardbusiness.org, or mailed to
Permissions, Harvard Business School Publishing, 60 Harvard Way,
Boston, Massachusetts 02163.

The *Harvard Business Review* articles in this collection are available as
individual reprints. Discounts apply to quantity purchases. For information and ordering, please contact Customer Service, Harvard Business
School Publishing, Boston, MA 02163. Telephone: (617) 783-7500 or
(800) 988-0886, 8 A.M. to 6 P.M. Eastern Time, Monday through Friday.
Fax: (617) 783-7555, 24 hours a day. E-mail:
custserv@harvardbusiness.org.

978-1-59139-768-7 (ISBN 13)
Library of Congress Cataloging-in-Publication Data
Harvard business review on appraising employee performance.
        p.   cm. — (The Harvard business review paperback series)
    Includes index.
    ISBN 1-59139-768-5
    1. Employees—Rating of. 2. Performance standards. 2. Personnel
management. I. Harvard business review. II. Series.
HF5549.5.R3H3 2005
658.3´125—dc22   2004016976
                                                                    CIP

Contents

Harvard Business Review

ON

APPRAISING EMPLOYEE PERFORMANCE

Management by
Whose Objectives?

HARRY LEVINSON

Executive Summary

IN THIS 1970 CLASSIC HBR ARTICLE, Levinson shares practical insights into the mysteries of motivation and takes a fresh look at the use and abuse of the most powerful tools for inspiring and guiding complex organizations. He argues that to motivate people successfully, management must focus on the question, "How do we meet both individual and organizational requirements?" When we make assumptions about individual motivations and increase pressure based on them, we ignore the fact that people work to meet their own psychological needs. Commitment must derive from the individual's wishes to support the organization's goals.

The performance appraisal systems that underpin management by objectives (MBO) fail to take into account the deeper emotional components of motivation. Instead, managers are forced to commit to unrealistic goals. Superiors are profoundly uncomfortable rating people on performance, and they execute this important task poorly. The individual's desires are entirely absent from most performance measurement systems; managers assume that these desires are perfectly aligned with corporate goals and that if they're not, the individual should move on.

Self-motivation occurs when individual needs and organizational requirements converge. However, successful management systems begin with the *employee's* objectives. The manager's task is to understand the employee's needs and then, with the employee, assess how well the organization can meet them. Objectives lack significant incentive power if they are unrelated to employees' underlying personal aspirations. Management should give more weight to areas of discretion open to the individual but not officially incorporated into job descriptions or goals. Otherwise, a person may objectively do an excellent job but still fail as a partner, subordinate, superior, or colleague.

DESPITE THE FACT THAT the concept of management by objectives (MBO) has by this time become an integral part of the managerial process, the typical MBO effort perpetuates and intensifies hostility, resentment, and distrust between a manager and subordinates. As currently practiced, it is really just industrial engineering with a new name, applied to higher managerial levels, and with the same resistances intact.

Obviously, somewhere between the concept of MBO and its implementation, something has seriously gone wrong. Coupled with performance appraisal, the intent is to follow the Frederick Taylor tradition of a more rational management process. That is, which people are to do what, who is to have effective control over the process, and how compensation is to be related directly to individual achievement. The MBO process, in its essence, is an effort to be fair and reasonable, to predict performance and judge it more carefully, and presumably to provide individuals with an opportunity to be self-motivating by setting their own objectives.

The intent of clarifying job obligations and measuring performance against an employee's own goals seems reasonable enough. The concern for having superior and subordinate consider the same matters in reviewing the performance of the latter is eminently sensible. The effort to come to common agreement on what constitutes the subordinate's job is highly desirable.

Yet, like most rationalizations in the Taylor tradition, MBO as a process is one of the greatest of managerial illusions because it fails to take adequately into account the deeper emotional components of motivation.

In this article, I shall indicate how I think management by objectives, as it is currently practiced in most organizations, is self-defeating and serves simply to increase pressure on the individual. By doing so, I am not rejecting either MBO or performance appraisal out of hand.

Rather, by raising the basic question, "Whose objectives?" I propose to suggest how they might be made into more constructive devices for effective management. The issues I shall raise have largely to do with psychological considerations, and particularly with the assumptions about motivation that underlie these techniques.

The "Ideal" Process

Because management by objectives is closely related to performance appraisal and review, I shall consider these together as one practice, which is intended:

- To measure and judge performance,

- To relate individual performance to organizational goals,

- To clarify both the job to be done and the expectations of accomplishment,

- To foster the increasing competence and growth of the subordinate,

- To enhance communications between superior and subordinate,

- To serve as a basis for judgments about salary and promotion,

- To stimulate the subordinate's motivation, and

- To serve as a device for organizational control and integration.

MAJOR PROBLEMS

According to contemporary thinking, the "ideal" process should proceed in five steps: 1) individual discussion with the superior of the subordinate's own job description, 2) establishment of the employee's short-term performance targets, 3) meetings with the superior to discuss the employee's progress toward targets, 4) establishment of checkpoints to measure progress, and 5) discussion between superior and subordinate at the end of a defined period to assess the results of the subordinate's efforts. In ideal practice, this process occurs against a background of more frequent, even day-to-day, contacts and is separate from salary review. But, in actual practice, there are many problems:

No matter how detailed the job description, it is essentially static—that is, a series of statements. However, the more complex the task and the more flexible an employee must be in it, the less any fixed statement of job elements will fit what that person does. Thus, the higher a person rises in an organization and the more varied and subtle the work, the more difficult it is to pin down objectives that represent more than a fraction of his or her effort.

With preestablished goals and descriptions, little weight can be given to the areas of discretion open to the individual but not incorporated into a job description or objectives. I am referring here to those spontaneously creative activities an innovative executive might choose to do, or those tasks a responsible executive sees need to be done. As we move toward a service society, in which tasks are less well defined but spontaneity of service and self-assumed responsibility are crucial, this becomes pressing.

Most job descriptions are limited to what employees do in their work. They do not adequately take into account the increasing interdependence of managerial work in organizations. This limitation becomes more important as the impact of social and organizational factors on individual performance becomes better understood. The more employees' effectiveness depends on what other people do, the less any one employee can be held responsible for the outcome of individual efforts.

If a primary concern in performance review is counseling the subordinate, appraisal should consider and take into account the total situation in which the superior and subordinate are operating. In addition, this should take into account the relationship of the subordinate's job to other jobs. In counseling, much of the focus is on helping the subordinate learn to negotiate the system. There is no provision in most reviews and no place on appraisal forms with which I am familiar to report and record such discussion.

The setting and evolution of objectives is done over too brief a period of time to provide for adequate interaction among different levels of an organization. This militates against opportunity for peers, both in the same work unit and in complementary units, to develop objectives together for maximum integration. Thus, both the setting of objectives and the appraisal of performance make little contribution to the development of teamwork and more effective organizational self-control.

Coupled with these problems is the difficulty that superiors experience when they undertake appraisals. Douglas McGregor complained that the major reason appraisal failed was that superiors disliked playing God by making judgments about another person's worth.[1] He likened the superior's experience to inspection of assembly-line products and contended that his revulsion was against being inhuman. To cope with this problem, McGregor recommended that an individual should set his or her own goals, checking them out with the superior, and should use the appraisal session as a counseling device. Thus, the superior would become one who helped subordinates achieve their own goals instead of a dehumanized inspector of products.

Parenthetically, I doubt very much that the failure of appraisal stems from playing God or feeling inhuman. My own observation leads me to believe that managers experience their appraisal of others as a hostile, aggressive act that unconsciously is felt to be hurting or destroying the other person. The appraisal situation, therefore, gives rise to powerful, paralyzing feelings of guilt that make it extremely difficult for most executives to be constructively critical of subordinates.

OBJECTIVITY PLEA

Be that as it may, the more complex and difficult the appraisal process and the setting and evaluation of objectives, the more pressing the cry for objectivity. This is a vain plea. Every organization is a social system, a network of interpersonal relationships. A person may do an excellent job by objective standards of measurement, but may fail miserably as a partner, subordinate, superior, or colleague. It is a commonplace that more people fail to be promoted for personal reasons than for technical inadequacy.

Furthermore, because all subordinates are a component of their superiors' efforts to achieve their own goals, subordinates will inevitably be appraised on how well they work with superiors and help the latter meet goals. A heavy subjective element necessarily enters into every appraisal and goal-setting experience.

The plea for objectivity is made in vain for another reason. The greater the emphasis placed on measurement and quantification, the more likely the subtle, nonmeasurable elements of the task will be sacrificed. Quality of performance frequently, therefore, loses out to quantification.

A case example. One manufacturing plant that produces high-quality, high-prestige products, backed by a reputation for customer consideration and service, has instituted an MBO program. It is well worked out and has done much to clarify individual goals and organizational performance. It is an important component of the professional management style of that company, which has resulted in commendable growth.

But an interesting, and ultimately destructive, process has been set in motion. The managers are beginning to worry because now when they ask why something has not been done, they hear from one another, "That isn't in my goals." They complain that customer service is deteriorating. The vague goal, "improve customer service," is almost impossible to measure. There is therefore heavy concentration on those subgoals that can be measured. Thus, time per customer, number of customer calls, and similar measures are used as guides in judging performance. The less time per customer and the fewer the calls, the better the customer service manager meets his objectives. He is cutting costs, increasing profit—and killing the business. Worse still, he hates himself.

Most of the managers in that organization joined it because of its reputation for high quality and good service. They want to make good products and earn the continued admiration of their customers, as well as the envy of their industry. When they are not operating at that high level, they feel guilty. They become angry with themselves and the company. They feel that they might just as well be working for someplace else that admittedly does a sloppy job of quality control and could hardly care less about service.

The same problem exists with respect to the development of personnel, which is another vague goal that is hard to measure in comparison with subgoals that are measurable. If asked, each manager can name a younger employee as a potential successor, particularly if a promotion depends on doing so; but no one has the time, or indeed is being paid, to thoroughly train the younger person. Nor can one have the time or be paid, for there is no way in that organization to measure how well a manager does in developing another.

The Missed Point

All of the problems with objectives and appraisals outlined in the example discussed in the foregoing section indicate that MBO is not working well despite what some companies think about their programs. The underlying reason it is not working well is that it misses the whole human point.

To see how the point is being missed, let us follow the typical MBO process. Characteristically, top management sets its corporate goal for the coming year. This may be in terms of return on investment, sales, production, growth, or other measurable factors.

Within this frame of reference, reporting managers may then be asked how much their units intend to contribute toward meeting that goal, or they may be asked to set their own goals relatively independent of the corporate goal. If they are left free to set their own goals, these in any case are expected to be higher than those they had the previous year. Usually, each reporting manager's range of choices is limited to an option for a piece of the organizational action or improvement of specific statistics. In some cases, it may also include obtaining specific training or skills.

Once a reporting manager decides on the unit's goals and has them approved by his superior, those become the manager's goals. Presumably, he has committed himself to what he wants to do. He has said it and he is responsible for it. He is thereafter subject to being hoisted with his own petard.

Now, let us reexamine this process closely: The whole method is based on a short-term, egocentrically oriented perspective and an underlying reward-punishment psychology. The typical MBO process puts the reporting manager in much the same position as a rat in a maze, which has choices between only two alternatives. The experimenter who puts the rat in the maze assumes that the rat will choose the food reward. If that cannot be presumed, the rat is starved to make sure it wants the food.

Management by objectives differs only in that it permits the manager to determine his or her own bait from a limited range of choices. Having done so, the MBO process assumes that the manager will a) work hard to get it, b) be pushed internally by reason of this commitment, and c) be responsible to the organization for doing so.

In fairness to most managers, they certainly try, but not without increasing resentment and complaint for feeling like rats in a maze, guilt for not paying attention to those parts of the job not in their objectives, and passive resistance to the mounting pressure for ever-higher goals.

PERSONAL GOALS

The MBO process leaves out the answers to such questions as: What are the managers' personal objectives?

What do they need and want out of their work? How do their needs and wants change from year to year? What relevance do organizational objectives and their part in them have to such needs and wants?

Obviously, no objectives will have significant incentive power if they are forced choices unrelated to a person's underlying dreams, wishes, and personal aspirations.

For example: If a salesperson relishes the pleasure of his relationships with his hard-earned but low-volume customers, this is a powerful need for him. Suppose his boss, who is concerned about increasing the volume of sales, urges him to concentrate on the larger-quantity customers rather than the smaller ones, which will provide the necessary increase in volume, and then asks him how much of an increase he can achieve.

To work with the larger-quantity customers means that he will be less likely to sell to the individuals with whom he has well-established relationships and be more likely to deal with purchasing agents, technical people, and staff specialists who will demand of him knowledge and information he may not have in sophisticated detail. Moreover, as a single salesperson, his organization may fail to support him with technical help to meet these demands.

When this happens, not only may he lose his favorite way of operating, which has well served his own needs, but he may have demands put on him that cause him to feel inadequate. If he is being compelled to make a choice about the percent of sales volume increase he expects to attain, he may well do that, but now he's under great psychological pressure. No one has recognized the psychological realities he faces, let alone helped him to work with them. It is simply assumed that because his sales goal is a rational one, he will see its rationality and pursue it.

The problem may be further compounded if, as is not unusual, formal changes are made in the organizational structure. If sales territories are shifted, if problems of delivery occur, if modes of compensation are changed, or whatever, all of these are factors beyond the salesperson's control. Nevertheless, even with certain allowances, he is still held responsible for meeting his sales goal.

PSYCHOLOGICAL NEEDS

Lest the reader think that the example we have just seen is overdrawn or irrelevant, I know of a young sales manager who is about to resign his job, despite success in it, because he chooses not to be expendable in an organization that he feels regards him only as an instrument for reaching a goal. Many young people are refusing to enter large organizations for just this reason.

Some may argue that my criticism is unfair, that many organizations start their planning and setting of objectives from below. Therefore, the company cannot be accused of putting a person in a maze. But it does so. In almost all cases, the only legitimate objectives to be set are those having to do with measurable increases in performance. This highlights, again, the question, "Whose objectives?" The question becomes more pressing in those circumstances where lower-level people set their objectives, only to be questioned by higher-level managers and told their targets are not high enough.

You may well ask, "What's the matter with that? Aren't we in business, and isn't the purpose of the employee's work to serve the requirements of the business?" The answer to both questions is, "Obviously." But that is only part of the story.

If a person's most powerful driving force is comprised of needs, wishes, and personal aspirations, combined with the compelling wish to look good in her own eyes for meeting those deeply held personal goals, then management by objectives should begin with *her* objectives. What does she want to do with her life? Where does she want to go? What will make her feel good about herself? What does she want to be able to look back on when she has expended her unrecoverable years?

At this point, some may say that those are her business. The company has other business, and it must assume that the employee is interested in working in the company's business rather than her own. That kind of differentiation is impossible. Everyone is always working toward meeting his or her psychological needs. Anyone who thinks otherwise, and who believes such powerful internal forces can be successfully disregarded or bought off for long, is deluded.

The Mutual Task

The organizational task becomes one of first understanding the employee's needs, and then, with him or her, assessing how well they can be met in this organization, doing what the organization needs to have done. Thus, the highest point of self-motivation arises when there is a complementary conjunction of the individual's needs and the organization's requirements. The requirements of both mesh, interrelate, and become synergistic. The energies of employee and organization are pooled for mutual advantage.

If the two sets of needs do not mesh, then a person has to fight him- or herself and the organization, in addition to the work that must be done and the targets that have been defined. In such a case, this requires the subordinate and the boss to evaluate together where the employee wants to go, where the organization is going, and how significant the discrepancy is. This person might well be better off somewhere else, and the organization would do better to have someone else in place whose needs mesh better with the organization's requirements.

LONG-RUN COSTS

The issue of meshed interests is particularly relevant for middle-aged, senior-level managers.[2] As people come into middle age, their values often begin to change, and they feel anew the pressure to accomplish many long-deferred dreams. When such wishes begin to stir, they begin to experience severe conflict.

Up to this point, they have committed themselves to the organization and have done sufficiently well in it to attain high rank. Usually, they are slated for even higher levels of responsibility. The organization has been good to them, and their superiors are depending on them to provide its leadership. They have been models for the younger employees, whom they have urged to aspire to organizational heights. To think of leaving is to desert both their superiors and their subordinates.

Because there are few avenues within the organization to talk about such conflict, these managers try to suppress their wishes. The internal pressure continues to mount until they finally make an impulsive break, surprising and dismaying both themselves and their colleagues. I can think of three vice presidents who have done just that.

The issue is not so much that they decide to leave, but the cost of the way they depart. Early discussion with superiors of their personal goals would have enabled both to examine possible relocation alternatives within the organization. If there were none, then both the managers and their superiors might have come to an earlier, more comfortable decision about separation. The organization would have had more time to make satisfactory alternative plans, as well as to have taken steps to compensate for the manager's lagging enthusiasm. Lower-level managers would then have seen the company as humane in its enlightened self-interest and would not have had to create fearful fantasies about what the top management conflicts were that had caused a good person to leave.

To place consideration of the managers' personal objectives first does not minimize the importance of the organization's goals. It does not mean there is anything wrong with the organization's need to increase its return on investment, its size, its productivity, or its other goals. However, I contend that it is ridiculous to make assumptions about the motivations of individuals, and then to set up means of increasing the pressures on people based on these often questionable assumptions. While there may be certain demonstrable short-run statistical gains, what are the long-run costs?

One cost is that people may leave; another, that they may fall back from competitive positions to plateaus. Why should an individual be expendable for someone else and sacrifice for something that is not a personal, cherished dream? Still another cost may be the loss of the essence of the business, as happened in the case example we saw earlier of the manufacturing plant with the problem of deteriorating customer service.

In that example, initially there was no dialogue. Nobody heard what the managers said, what they wanted, where they wanted to go, where they wanted the organization to go, and how they felt about the supposedly rational procedures that had been initiated. The underlying psychological assumption that management made unconsciously was that the managers had to be made more efficient; ergo, management by objectives.

Top management typically assumes that it alone has the prerogative to a) set the objectives, b) provide the rewards and targets, and c) drive anyone who works for the organization. As long as this reward-punishment psychology exists in any organization, the MBO appraisal process is certain to fail.

Many organizations are making this issue worse by promising young people they will have challenges because they assume these employees will be challenged by management's objectives. Managements are having difficulty, even when they have high turnover rates, hearing these youngsters say they could hardly care less for management's unilaterally determined objectives. Managements then become angry and complain that the young people do not want to work or that they want to become presidents overnight.

What the young people are asking is: What about me and my needs? Who will listen? How much will management help me meet my own requirements while also meeting its objectives?

The power of this force is reflected in the finding that the more a subordinate participates in the appraisal interview by presenting personal ideas and beliefs, the more likely he or she is to feel that a) the superior is helpful and constructive, b) some current job problems are being cleared up, and c) reasonable future goals are being set.[3]

Suggested Steps

Given the validity of all the MBO problems I have been discussing to this point, there are a number of possibilities for coping with them. Here, I suggest three beginning steps to consider.

MOTIVATIONAL ASSESSMENT

Every MBO program and its accompanying performance appraisal system should be examined as to the extent to which it a) expresses the conviction that people are patsies to be driven, urged, and manipulated, and b) fosters a genuine partnership between employee and organization, in which each has some influence over the other, as contrasted with a rat-in-maze relationship.

It is not easy for the nonpsychologist to answer such questions, but there are clues to the answers. One clue is how decisions about compensation, particularly bonuses, are made. For example: A sales manager asked for my judgment about an incentive plan for highly motivated salespeople who were in a seller's market. I asked why one was needed, and he responded, "To give them an incentive." When I pointed out that they were already highly motivated and apparently needed no incentive, he changed his rationale and said that the company wanted to share its success to keep the sales staff identified with it, and to express its recognition of their contribution.

I asked, "Why not let them establish the reward related to performance?" The question startled him; obviously, if they were going to decide, who needed him? A fundamental aspect of his role, as he saw it, was to drive them ever onward, whether they needed it or not.

In a plastic-fabricating company, a middle-management bonus plan tied to performance proved to be highly unsatisfactory. Frustrated that its well-intentioned efforts were not working and determined to follow precepts of participative management,

ranking executives in the company involved many
people in formulating a new one: personnel, control,
marketing executives, and others—in fact, everyone
but the managers who were supposed to receive the
bonuses. Top management is now dismayed that the
new plan is as unsatisfactory as the old and bitter
that participation failed to work.

Another clue is the focus of company meetings. Some
are devoted to intensifying the competition between
units. Others lean heavily to exhortation and inspiration.
Contrast these orientations with meetings in which
people are apprised of problems and plan to cope with
them.

GROUP ACTION

Every objectives and appraisal program should include
group goal setting, group definition of individual
and group tasks, group appraisal of its accomplishments,
group appraisal of each individual member's contribution to the group effort (without basing compensation
on that appraisal), and shared compensation based on
the relative success with which group goals are achieved.
Objectives should include long-term as well as short-
term goals.

The rationale is simple. Every managerial job is an
interdependent task. Managers have responsibilities to
one another as well as to their superiors. The reason for
having an organization is to achieve more together than
each could alone. Why, then, emphasize and reward individual performance alone, based on static job descriptions? That approach can only orient people to incorrect
and self-centered goals.

Therefore, where people are in complementary relationships, whether they report to the same superior or

not, both horizontal and vertical goal formulation should be formalized, with regular, frequent opportunity for review of problems and progress. They should help one another define and describe their respective jobs, enhancing control and integration at the point of action.

In my judgment, for example, a group of managers (sales, promotion, advertising) reporting to a vice president of marketing should formulate their collective goals and define ways of helping one another and of assessing one another's effectiveness in the common task. The group assessment of each manager's work should be a means of providing each one with constructive feedback, not for determining pay. However, in addition to their salaries, they should each receive, as part of whatever additional compensation is offered, a return based on the group effort.

The group's discussion among itself and with its superior should include examination of organizational and environmental obstacles to goal achievement, and particularly of what organizational and leadership supports are required to attain objectives. One important reason for this is that often people think there are barriers where none would exist if they initiated action. ("You mean the president really wants us to get together and solve this problem?")

Another reason is that frequently when higher management sets goals, it is unaware of significant barriers to achievement, which makes managers cynical. For example, if there is no comprehensive orientation and support program to help new employees adapt, then pressure on lower-level managers to employ disadvantaged minority group members and to reduce their turnover can only be experienced by those managers as hollow mockery.

APPRAISAL OF APPRAISERS

Every management by objectives and appraisal program should include regular appraisals of the manager by subordinates, and be reviewed by the manager's superior. Every manager should be specifically compensated for how well he or she develops people, based on such appraisals. The very phrase "reporting to" reflects the fact that although a manager has a responsibility, the superior also has a responsibility for what he or she does and how it's done.

In fact, both common sense and research indicate that the single most significant outside influence on how a manager performs is the superior. If that is the case, then the key environmental factor in task accomplishment and managerial growth is the relationship between manager and superior.

Therefore, objectives should include not only the individual manager's personal and occupational goals, but also the corporate goals manager and superior share in common. They should together appraise their relationship vis-à-vis both the manager's individual goals and their joint objectives, review what they have done together, and discuss its implications for their next joint steps.

A manager rarely is in a position to judge a superior's overall performance, but he or she can appraise how well the superior has helped the manager to do the job, how well the superior is helping to increase the manager's proficiency and visibility, what problems the superior poses for the manager, and what kinds of support the superior can use. Such feedback serves several purposes.

Most important, it offers some guidance on the superior's own managerial performance. In addition, and particularly when the manager is protected by higher-level review of this appraisal, it provides the supervisor with direct feedback on his or her own behavior. This is much more constructive than behind-the-back complaints and vituperative terminal interviews, in which cases there is no opportunity either for self-defense or corrective behavior. Every professional counselor has had recently fired executive clients who did not know why they had been discharged for being poor superiors when, according to their information, their subordinates thought so much of them. In his or her own self-interest, every manager should want appraisal by subordinates.

The Basic Consideration

When the three organizational conditions we have just seen do in fact exist, then it is appropriate to think of starting management by objectives with a consideration of each employee's personal objectives; if the underlying attitude in the organization toward the subordinate is that he or she is but an object, there is certainly no point in starting with the person. Nor is there any point in trying to establish confidence in superiors when there is no protection from their rivalry, or being pitted against peers. Anyone who expressed personal fears and innermost wishes under these circumstances would be a damned fool.

For reasons I have already indicated, it should be entirely legitimate in every business for these concerns to be the basis for setting individual objectives. This is because the fundamental managerial consideration necessarily must be focused on the question: "How do we meet both individual and organizational purposes?" If a major intention of management by objectives is to enlist the self-motivated commitment of the individual, then that commitment must derive from the individual's powerful wishes to support the organization's goals; otherwise, the commitment will be incidental to any personal wishes.

Having said that, the real difficulty begins. How can any superior know what a subordinate's personal goals and wishes are if even the subordinate—as most of us are—is not clear about them? How ethical is it for a superior to pry into an employee's personal life? How can he or she keep from forming a negative judgment about someone who is losing interest in work, or is not altogether identified with the company? How can the superior keep that knowledge from interfering with judgments he or she might otherwise make, and opportunities he or she might otherwise offer? How often are the personal goals, particularly in middle age, temporary fantasies that are better not discussed? Can a superior who is untrained in psychology handle such information constructively? Will he or she perhaps do more harm than good?

These are critically important questions. They deserve careful thought. My answers should be taken as no more than beginning steps.

EGO CONCEPTS

Living is a process of constant adaptation. An individual's personal goals, wishes, and aspirations are continuously evolving and being continuously modified by experiences. That is one reason why it is so difficult for an individual to specify concrete personal objectives.

Nevertheless, each of us has a built-in road map, a picture of his or her future best self. Psychologists speak of this as an *ego ideal*, which is comprised of a person's values, the expectations parents and others have held out for competences and skills, and favorite ways of behaving. An ego ideal is essentially the way an individual thinks he or she ought to be. Much of a person's ego ideal is unconscious, which is another reason why it is not clear.

Subordinates' self-examination. Although people cannot usually spell out their ego ideal, they can talk about those experiences that have been highly gratifying, even exhilarating. They can specify those rare peak experiences that made them feel very good about themselves. When they have an opportunity to talk about what they have found especially gratifying and also what they think would be gratifying to them, people are touching on central elements of their ego ideal.

Given the opportunity to talk about such experiences and wishes on successive occasions, people can begin to spell out for themselves the central thrust of their lives. Reviewing all of the occupational choices they have made and the reasons for making them, people can begin to see the common threads in those choices and therefore the momentum of their personalities. As these become clearer, they are in a better position to weigh alternatives against the mainstream of their personalities.

For example, an individual who has successively chosen occupational alternatives in which she was individually competitive, and whose most exhilarating experiences have come from defeating an opponent or single-handedly vanquishing a problem, would be unlikely to find a staff position exhilarating, no matter what it paid or what it was called. Her ideal for herself is that of a vanquishing, competitive person.

The important concept here is that it is not necessary that an individual spell out concrete goals at any one point; rather, it is helpful to both the individual and the organization if he or she is able to examine and review aloud on a continuing basis personal thoughts and feelings in relation to his or her work. Such a process makes it legitimate to bring his or her own feelings to consciousness and talk about them in the business context as the basis for a relationship to the organization.

By listening, and helping the subordinate to spell out how and what he or she feels, the superior does not do anything to the subordinate, and therefore by that self-appraisal process cannot be hurtful. The information serves both employee and superior as a criterion for examining the relationship of the employee's feelings and, however dimly perceived, personal goals to organizational goals. Even if some of these wishes and aspirations are mere fantasy and impossible to gratify, if it is legitimate to talk about them without being laughed at, the individual can compare them with the realities of his or her life and make more reasonable choices.

Even in the safest organizational atmosphere, for reasons already mentioned, it will not be easy for managers to talk about their goals. The best-intentioned supervisor is likely to be something less than a highly skilled interviewer. These two facts suggest that any effort to ascertain a subordinate's personal goals is futile; but I think not.

The important point is not the specificity of the statement that any person can make, but the nature of a superior-subordinate relationship that makes it safe to explore such feelings and gives first consideration to the individual. In such a context, both subordinate and superior may come closer to evolving an employee-organization fit than they might otherwise.

Superior's introspection. An employee-organization relationship requires the superior to engage in some introspection, too. Suppose he has prided himself on bringing along a bright young manager who, he now learns, is thinking of moving into a different field. How can he keep from being angry and disappointed? How can he cope with the conflict he now faces when it is time to make recommendations for advancement or a raise?

The superior cannot keep from being angry and disappointed. Such feelings are natural in that circumstance. He can express feelings of disappointment to his protégé without being critical of the latter. But, if he continues to feel angry, then he needs to ask himself why another person's assertion of independence irritates him so. The issues of advancement and raises should continue to be based on the same realistic premises as they would have been before.

Of course, it now becomes appropriate to consider with the individual whether—in view of his feelings—he wants to take on the burden of added responsibility and can reasonably discharge it. If he thinks he does, and can, he is likely to pursue the new responsibility with added determination. With his occupational choice conflict no longer hidden, and with fewer feelings of guilt about it, his commitment to his chosen alternative is likely to be more intense.

And if an employee has earned a raise, he or she should get it. To withhold it merely punishes him or her, which puts the relationship back on a reward-punishment basis.

The question of how ethical it is to conduct such discussions as part of a business situation hinges on the climate of the organization and on the sense of personal responsibility of each executive. Where the organization's ethos is one of building trust and keeping confidences, there is no reason why executives cannot be as ethical as lawyers or physicians.

If the individual executive cannot be trusted in relationships with subordinates, then he or she cannot have their respect or confidence in any case, and the ordinary MBO appraisal process simply serves as a management pressure device. If the organization's ethos is one of rapacious internal competition, backbiting, and distrust, there is little point in talking about self-motivation, human needs, or commitment.

Management by objectives and performance appraisal processes, as typically practiced, are inherently self-defeating over the long run because they are based on a reward-punishment psychology that serves to intensify the pressure on the individual while really offering a very limited choice of objectives. Such processes can be improved by examining the psychological assumptions underlying them, by extending them to include group appraisal and appraisal of superiors by subordinates, and by considering the personal goals of the individual first. These practices require a high level of ethical standards and personal responsibility in the organization.

Such appraisal processes would diminish the feeling on the part of the superior that appraisal is a hostile, destructive act. While superior and subordinate would still have to judge the latter's individual performance, this judgment would occur in a context of continuing consideration for personal needs and reappraisal of organizational and environmental realities.

Not having to be continuously on the defensive and aware of the organization's genuine interest in having him or her meet personal as well as organizational goals, a manager would be freer to evaluate him- or herself against what has to be done. Because there would be many additional frames of reference in both horizontal and vertical goal setting, the manager would need no longer feel under appraisal, attack, or judgment as an isolated individual against the system. Furthermore, there would be multiple modes for contributing ideas and a varied method for exerting influence upward and horizontally.

In these contexts, too, the manager could raise questions and concerns about qualitative aspects of performance. Then manager, colleagues, and superiors could together act to cope with such issues without the barrier of having to consider only statistics. Thus, a continuing process of interchange would counteract the problem of the static job description and provide multiple avenues for feedback on performance and joint action.

In such an organizational climate, work relationships would then become dynamic networks for both personal and organizational achievements. A not-incidental gain from such arrangements is that problems would more likely be solved spontaneously at the lowest possible levels, and free superiors simultaneously from the burden of the passed buck and the onus of being the purveyors of hostility.

Notes

1. "An Uneasy Look at Performance Appraisal," HBR May–June 1957, p. 89. (Reprinted as an HBR Classic, September–October 1972.)

2. See my article, "On Being a Middle-Aged Manager," HBR July–August 1969, p. 51.

3. Ronald J. Burke and Douglas S. Wilcox, "Characteristics of Effective Employee Performance Reviews and Developmental Interviews," *Personal Psychology,* Vol. 22, No. 3, 1969, p. 291.

Originally published in July–August 1970
Reprint R0301H

Fear of Feedback

JAY M. JACKMAN AND MYRA H. STROBER

Executive Summary

NOBODY LIKES performance reviews. Subordinates are terrified they'll hear nothing but criticism. Bosses think their direct reports will respond to even the mildest criticism with anger or tears. The result? Everyone keeps quiet. That's unfortunate, because most people need help figuring out how to improve their performance and advance their careers.

This fear of feedback doesn't come into play just during annual reviews. At least half the executives with whom the authors have worked *never* ask for feedback. Many expect the worst: heated arguments, even threats of dismissal. So rather than seek feedback, people try to guess what their bosses are thinking.

Fears and assumptions about feedback often manifest themselves in psychologically maladaptive behaviors such as procrastination, denial, brooding, jealousy, and self-sabotage. But there's hope, say the authors. Those who learn adaptive techniques can free themselves from destructive responses. They'll be able to deal with feedback better if they acknowledge negative emotions, reframe fear and criticism constructively, develop realistic goals, create support systems, and reward themselves for achievements along the way.

Once you've begun to alter your maladaptive behaviors, you can begin seeking regular feedback from your boss. The authors take you through four steps for doing just that: self-assessment, external assessment, absorbing the feedback, and taking action toward change.

Organizations profit when employees ask for feedback and deal well with criticism. Once people begin to know how they are doing relative to management's priorities, their work becomes better aligned with organizational goals. What's more, they begin to transform a feedback-averse environment into a more honest and open one, in turn improving performance throughout the organization.

Nobody likes performance reviews. Subordinates are terrified they'll hear nothing but criticism. Bosses, for their part, think their direct reports will respond to even the mildest criticism with stonewalling, anger, or tears. The result? Everyone keeps quiet and says as little as possible. That's unfortunate, because most people need help figuring out how they can improve their performance and advance their careers.

This fear of feedback doesn't come into play just during annual reviews. At least half the executives with whom we've worked *never* ask for feedback. Many expect the worst: heated arguments, impossible demands, or even threats of dismissal. So rather than seek feedback, people avoid the truth and instead continue to try to guess what their bosses think.

Fears and assumptions about feedback often manifest themselves in psychologically maladaptive behaviors such as procrastination, denial, brooding, jealousy, and self-sabotage. But there's hope. Those who learn to adapt to feedback can free themselves from old patterns. They can learn to acknowledge negative emotions, constructively reframe fear and criticism, develop realistic goals, create support systems, and reward themselves for achievements along the way.

We'll look closely at a four-step process for doing just that. But before we turn to that process, let's explore why so many people are afraid to hear how they're doing.

Fear Itself

Obviously, some managers have excellent relationships with their bosses. They receive feedback on a regular basis and act on it in ways that improve their performance as well as their prospects for promotion. Sadly, however, such executives are in the minority. In most companies, feedback typically comes via cursory annual performance reviews, during which managers learn little beyond the amount of a forthcoming raise.

People avoid feedback because they hate being criticized, plain and simple. Psychologists have a lot of theories about why people are so sensitive to hearing about their own imperfections. One is that they associate feedback with the critical comments received in their younger years from parents and teachers. Whatever the cause of our discomfort, most of us have to train ourselves to seek feedback and listen carefully when we hear it. Absent that training, the very threat of critical feedback often leads us to practice destructive, maladaptive behaviors that negatively affect not only our work but the overall health of our organizations. The following are some examples of those behaviors.

PROCRASTINATION

We procrastinate—usually consciously—when we feel helpless about a situation and are anxious, embarrassed, or otherwise dissatisfied with it. Procrastination commonly contains an element of hostility or anger.

Consider how Joe, a highly accomplished computer scientist in a large technology company, responded to his frustration over not being promoted. (As with all the examples in this article, people's names have been changed.) Although everyone in the company respected his technical competence, he sensed something was wrong. Instead of seriously assessing his performance and asking for feedback, he became preoccupied with inessential details of his projects, played computer solitaire, and consistently failed to meet project deadlines. When Joe asked about his chances for advancement in his annual review, his boss singled out Joe's repeated failure to finish projects on time or to seek formal extensions when he knew work would be late. In fact, Joe's continued procrastination became a serious performance issue that cost him a promotion.

DENIAL

We're in denial when we're unable or unwilling to face reality or fail to acknowledge the implications of our situations. Denial is most often an unconscious response.

Angela, a midlevel manager in a consulting firm, drifted into a state of denial when a hoped-for promotion never materialized. Her superiors told her that she hadn't performed as well as they'd expected. Specifically, they told her she'd requested too much time off to spend with her children, she hadn't sufficiently researched a certain industry, she hadn't met her yearly quota of bringing in ten new clients, and so on. Every time she tried to correct these problems, her male superiors put her off with a new series of excuses and challenges. The fact was, they had no intention of promoting her because they were deeply sexist. Accepting that fact would have required Angela to leave, but she chose instead to live in denial. Rather than recognize she was at a dead end, she did nothing about her situation and remained miserable in her job.

BROODING

Brooding is a powerful emotional response, taking the form of morbid preoccupation and a sense of foreboding. Faced with situations they feel they can't master, brooders lapse into assivity, paralysis, and isolation.

Adrian, a training manager, brooded when his boss set forth several stretch goals for him. Believing the goals to be unrealistic, Adrian concluded that he couldn't meet them. Rather than talk with his boss about this, he became desperately unhappy and withdrew from his colleagues. They in turn saw his withdrawal as a snub and began to ignore him. The more they avoided him, the more he brooded. By the end of six months, Adrian's brooding created a self-fulfilling prophecy; because he had met none of his goals, his new projects were assigned to someone else, and his job was in jeopardy.

JEALOUSY

Comparing ourselves with others is a normal behavior, but it becomes maladaptive when it is based on suspicion, rivalry, envy, or possessiveness. Jealous people may overidealize others whom they perceive to be more talented, competent, and intelligent; in so doing, they debilitate themselves.

Leslie, a talented vice president of a public relations firm, fell into the jealousy trap when her boss noted during a meeting that one of her colleagues had prepared a truly excellent report for a client. Leslie began comparing herself with her colleague, listening carefully to the boss's remarks during meetings and noting his smiles and nods as he spoke. Feeling that she could never rise to her colleague's level, Leslie lost all enthusiasm for her work. Instead of seeking a reality check with her boss, she allowed the green-eyed monster to consume her; ultimately, she quit her job.

SELF-SABOTAGE

Examples of self-sabotage, usually an unconscious behavior, are all too common. Even national leaders such as Bill Clinton and Trent Lott have hoisted themselves on their own petards.

Workplaces are full of people who unconsciously undercut themselves. Take, for example, the story of Nancy, a young associate who found herself unable to deal with more than two projects at once. During her review, Nancy resented her boss's feedback that she needed to improve her ability to multitask. But instead of initiating further discussion with him about the remark, she "accidentally" made a nasty comment about him one day within his earshot. As a result, he began looking for ways to get rid of her. When she was eventually fired, her innermost feelings of unworthiness were validated.

These and other maladaptive behaviors are part of a vicious cycle we have seen at play in too many organizations. Indeed, it's not uncommon for employees, faced with negative feedback, to rain private maledictions upon their supervisors. No wonder, then, that supervisors are reluctant to give feedback. But when employees' imagined and real fears go unchecked, the work environment becomes dysfunctional, if not downright poisonous.

Learning to Adapt

Adapting to feedback—which inevitably asks people to change, sometimes significantly—is critical for managers who find themselves in jobs, companies, and industries undergoing frequent transitions. Of course, adaptation is easier said than done, for resistance to change is endemic in human beings. But while most people feel they can't control the negative emotions that are aroused by change, this is not the case. It is possible—and necessary—to think positively about change. Using the following adaptive techniques, you can alter how you respond to feedback and to the changes it demands.

RECOGNIZE YOUR EMOTIONS AND RESPONSES

Understanding that you are experiencing fear ("I'm afraid my boss will fire me") and that you are exhibiting a maladaptive response to that fear ("I'll just stay out of his way and keep my mouth shut") are the critical initial steps toward adaptive change. They require ruthless self-honesty and a little detective work, both of which will go a long way toward helping you undo years of disguising your feelings. It's important to understand, too, that a particular maladaptive behavior does not necessarily tell you what emotion underlies it: You may be procrastinating out of anger, frustration, sadness, or other feelings. But persevering in the detective work is important, for the payoff is high. Having named the emotion and response, you can then act—just as someone who fears flying chooses to board a plane anyway. With practice, it gradually becomes easier to respond differently, even though the fear, anger, or sadness may remain.

Maria, a midlevel manager with whom we worked, is a good example of someone who learned to name her emotions and act despite them. Maria was several months overdue on performance reviews for the three people who reported to her. When we suggested that she was procrastinating, we asked her how she felt when she thought about doing the reviews. After some reflection, she said she was extremely resentful that her boss had not yet completed her own performance evaluation; she recognized that her procrastination was an expression of her anger toward him. We helped her realize that she could act despite her anger. Accordingly, Maria completed the performance evaluations for her subordinates and, in so doing, felt as if a huge weight had been lifted from her shoulders. Once she had completed the reviews, she noticed that her relationships with her three subordinates quickly improved, and her boss responded by finishing Maria's performance review.

We should note that Maria's procrastination was not an entrenched habit, so it was relatively easy to fix.

Employees who start procrastinating in response to negative emotions early in their work lives won't change that habit quickly—but they can eventually.

GET SUPPORT

Identifying your emotions is sometimes difficult, and feedback that requires change can leave you feeling inhibited and ashamed. For these reasons, it's critical to ask for help from trusted friends who will listen, encourage, and offer suggestions. Asking for support is often hard, because most corporate cultures expect managers to be self-reliant. Nevertheless, it's nearly impossible to make significant change without such encouragement. Support can come in many forms, but it should begin with at least two people—including, say, a spouse, a minister or spiritual counselor, a former mentor, an old high school classmate—with whom you feel emotionally safe. Ideally, one of these people should have some business experience. It may also help to enlist the assistance of an outside consultant or executive coach.

REFRAME THE FEEDBACK

Another adaptive technique, reframing, allows you to reconstruct the feedback process to your advantage. Specifically, this involves putting the prospect of asking for or reacting to feedback in a positive light so that negative emotions and responses lose their grip.

Take the example of Gary, a junior sales manager for a large manufacturing company. Gary's boss told him that he wasn't sociable enough with customers and prospects. The criticism stung, and Gary could have responded with denial or brooding. Indeed, his first response was to interpret the feedback as shallow. Eventually, though, Gary was able to reframe what he'd heard, first by grudgingly acknowledging it. ("He's right, I'm not very sociable. I tested as an introvert on the Myers-Briggs, and I've always been uncomfortable with small talk.") Then Gary reframed the feedback. Instead of seeing it as painful, he recognized that he could use it to help his career. Avoiding possible maladaptive responses, he was able to ask himself several important questions: "How critical is sociability to my position? How much do I want to keep this job? How much am I willing to change to become more sociable?" In responding, Gary realized two things: that sociability was indeed critical to success in sales and that he wasn't willing to learn to be more sociable. He requested a transfer and moved to a new position where he became much more successful.

BREAK UP THE TASK

Yet another adaptive technique is to divide up the large task of dealing with feedback into manageable, measurable chunks, and set realistic time frames for each one. Although more than two areas of behavior may need to be modified, it's our experience that most people can't change more than one or two at a time. Taking small steps and meeting discrete goals reduces your chances of being overwhelmed and makes change much more likely.

Jane, for example, received feedback indicating that the quality of her work was excellent but that her public presentations were boring. A quiet and reserved person, Jane could have felt overwhelmed by what she perceived as the subtext of this criticism: that she was a lousy public speaker and that she'd better transform

herself from a wallflower into a writer and actress.
Instead, she adapted by breaking down the challenge
of "interesting presentations" into its constituent parts
(solid and well-constructed content; a commanding
delivery; an understanding of the audience; and so on).
Then she undertook to teach herself to present more
effectively by observing several effective speakers and
taking an introductory course in public speaking.

It was important for Jane to start with the easiest
task—in this case, observing good speakers. She noted
their gestures, the organization of their speeches, their
intonation, timing, use of humor, and so forth. Once she
felt she understood what good speaking entailed, she was
ready to take the introductory speaking course. These
endeavors allowed her to improve her presentations.
Though she didn't transform herself into a mesmerizing
orator, she did learn to command the attention and
respect of an audience.

USE INCENTIVES

Pat yourself on the back as you make adaptive changes.
That may seem like unusual advice, given that feedback
situations can rouse us to self-punishment and few of us
are in the habit of congratulating ourselves. Nevertheless, nowhere is it written that the feedback process
must be a wholly negative experience. Just as a salary
raise or a bonus provides incentive to improve performance, rewarding yourself whenever you take an important step in the process will help you to persevere in your
efforts. The incentive should be commensurate with the
achievement. For example, an appropriate reward for
completing a self-assessment might be an uninterrupted
afternoon watching ESPN or, for a meeting with the boss,

a fine dinner out. (For a quick guide on learning to adapt, see the exhibit "Reframe Your Thinking.")

Getting the Feedback You Need

Once you've begun to adapt your responses and behavior, it's time to start seeking regular feedback from your boss rather than wait for the annual performance review to come around. The proactive feedback process we recommend consists of four manageable steps: self-assessment, external feedback, absorbing the feedback, and taking action toward change. The story of Bob, a vice president of human resources, illustrates how one executive used the four-step process to take charge of his work life.

When we first met Bob, he had been on the job for three years and felt he was in a feedback vacuum. Once a year, toward the end of December, Harry—the gruff, evasive CEO to whom he reported—would call Bob in, tell him what a fine job he had been doing, announce his salary for the following year, and give him a small bonus. But this year, Bob had been dealing with thorny issues— including complaints from senior female executives about unfair compensation—and needed some real feedback. Bob wondered how Harry viewed his work. Were there aspects of Bob's performance that Harry wasn't happy with? Did Harry intend to retain Bob in his current position?

SELF-ASSESSMENT

We encouraged Bob to begin by assessing his own performance. Self-assessment can be a tough assignment, particularly if one has never received useful feedback to begin with. The first task in self-assessment was for Bob to determine which elements of his job were most

Reframe Your Thinking

Almost everyone dreads performance reviews, which typically take place once a year. But how you respond to the boss's feedback—and how often you request it—will largely affect your performance and chances for career advancement. We've found that getting beyond that sense of dread involves recognizing and naming the emotions and behaviors that are preventing you from initiating feedback discussions. Once you determine those emotional and behavioral barriers, it's a matter of reframing your thoughts and moving toward more adaptive behavior. Below are some examples of how you might turn negative emotions into more positive, productive thoughts.

Possible Negative Emotion	Maladaptive Response	Reframing Statement
Anger (I'm mad at my boss because he won't talk to me directly.)	Acting out (stomping around, complaining, being irritable, yelling at subordinates or family)	It's up to me to get the feedback I need.
Anxiety (I don't know what will happen.)	Brooding (withdrawal, nail biting) Avoiding (I'm too busy to ask for feedback.)	Finding out can open up new opportunities for me.
Fear of confrontation (I don't want to do this.)	Denial, procrastination, self-sabotage (canceling meetings with boss)	Taking the initiative puts me in charge and gives me some power.
Fear of reprisal (If I speak up, will I get a pink slip?)	Denial (I don't need any feedback. I'm doing just fine.)	I really need to know honestly how I'm doing.
Hurt (Why did he say I wasn't trying hard enough?)	Irritability, jealousy of others (silence, plotting to get even)	I can still pay attention to what he said even though I feel hurt.
Defensiveness (I'm better than she says.)	Acting out by not supporting the boss (You can bet I'm not going to her stupid meeting.)	Being defensive keeps me from hearing what she has to say.
Sadness (I thought he liked me!)	Brooding, withdrawal (being quieter than usual, feeling demotivated)	How I'm doing in my job isn't about whether I'm liked.
Fear of change (How will I ever do all that he wants me to do?)	Denial (keep doing things the same way as before)	I must change to keep my job. I need to run the marathon one mile at a time.
Ambivalence (Should I stay or should I go?)	Procrastination, passivity (waiting for somebody else to solve the problem)	What really serves my interests best? Nobody is as interested in my well-being as I am. *I* need to take some action now.
Resignation (I have to leave!)	Resistance to change (It's just too hard to look for another job. It's not really so bad here.)	I'll be much happier working somewhere else.

important. The second was to recall informal feedback he had received from coworkers, subordinates, and customers—not only words, but facial expressions, body language, and silences.

Bob took several weeks to do his self-assessment. Once we helped him realize that he was procrastinating with the assessment, he enlisted a support system—his wife and an old college buddy—who encouraged him to finish his tally of recollections. At the end of the process, he recognized that he had received a good deal of positive informal feedback from many of the people with whom he interacted. But he also realized that he was too eager to please and needed to be more assertive in expressing his opinions. We helped him reframe these uncomfortable insights so that he could see them as areas for potential growth.

EXTERNAL FEEDBACK

The next phase of the proactive process—asking for feedback—is generally a two-part task: The first involves speaking to a few trusted colleagues to collect information that supports or revises your self-assessment. The second involves directly asking your boss for feedback. Gathering feedback from trusted colleagues shouldn't be confused with 360-degree feedback, which culls a wide variety of perspectives, including those from people who may not know you well. By speaking confidentially with people you genuinely trust, you can keep some of the fear associated with feedback at bay. Trusted colleagues can also help you identify your own emotional and possibly maladaptive responses to criticism, which is particularly beneficial prior to your meeting with your superior. Additionally, feedback conversations with colleagues can often serve as a form of dress rehearsal for the real thing. Sometimes, colleagues point out areas that warrant immediate attention; when they do, it's wise to make those changes before meeting with the boss. On the other hand, if you think you can't trust any of your colleagues, you should bypass such feedback conversations and move directly to setting up a meeting with your boss.

Bob asked for feedback from two trusted colleagues, Sheila and Paul, at meetings that he specifically scheduled for this purpose. He requested both positive and negative feedback and specific examples of areas in which he did well and in which he needed to improve. He listened intently to their comments, interrupting only for clarification. Both told him that he analyzed problems carefully and interacted well with employees. Yet Sheila noted that at particularly busy times of the year, Bob seemed to have difficulty setting his priorities, and Paul pointed out that Bob needed to be more assertive. Armed with his colleagues' feedback, Bob had a clearer notion of his strengths and weaknesses. He realized that some of his difficulties in setting priorities were owing to unclear direction from Harry, and he made a note to raise the matter with him.

The next step in external feedback—the actual meeting with your boss—requires delicate handling, particularly since the request may come as a surprise to him or her. In setting up the meeting, it's important to assure your boss that criticisms and suggestions will be heard, appreciated, and positively acted on. It's vital, too, to set the agenda for the meeting, letting your superior know that you have three or four questions based on your self-assessment and feedback from others. During the meeting, ask for specific examples and suggestions for change while remaining physically and emotionally neutral about the feedback you hear. Watch carefully not only for specific content but also for body language and tone, since feedback can be indirect as well as direct. When the meeting concludes, thank your boss and indicate that you will get back to her with a plan of action after you've had time to absorb what you've heard. Remember, too, that you can terminate the meeting if it becomes counterproductive (for example, if your boss responds to any of your questions with anger).

During his feedback meeting with Harry, Bob inquired about his work priorities. Harry told him that the company's financial situation looked precarious and that Bob should focus on locating and implementing a less costly health benefit plan. Harry warned Bob that a new plan would surely anger some employees, and because of that, Bob needed to develop a tougher skin to withstand the inevitable criticisms.

As Bob learned, feedback meetings can provide more than just a performance assessment; they can also offer some other important and unexpected insights. Bob had been so immersed in HR issues that he had never noted that Harry had been otherwise preoccupied with the company's financial problems.

ABSORBING THE FEEDBACK

Upon hearing critical feedback, you may well experience the negative emotions and maladaptive responses we described earlier. It's important to keep your reactions private until you can replace them with adaptive responses that lead to an appropriate plan of action.

Bob, for example, realized he felt irritated and vaguely hurt at the suggestion that he needed to toughen up. He brooded for a while but then reframed these feelings by recognizing that the negative feedback was as much a commentary on Harry's preoccupations as it was on Bob's performance. Bob didn't use the reframing to negate Harry's feedback; he accepted that he needed to be more assertive and hard-nosed in dealing with employees' issues.

TAKING ACTION

The last phase of the proactive feedback process involves coming to conclusions about, and acting on, the information you've received. Bob, for example, chose to focus on two action strategies: implementing a less costly health care plan—which included preparing himself to tolerate employee complaints—and quietly looking for new employment, since he now understood that the company's future was uncertain. Both of these decisions made Bob uncomfortable, for they evoked his fear of change. But having developed his adaptive responses, he no longer felt trapped by fear. In the months following, he implemented the new health benefits plan without taking his employees' criticisms personally. He also kept an eye on the company's financials and reconnected with his professional network in case it became clear the organization was starting to founder.

The Rewards of Adaptation

Organizations profit when executives seek feedback and are able to deal well with criticism. As executives begin to ask how they are doing relative to management's priorities, their work becomes better aligned with organizational goals. Moreover, as an increasing number of executives in an organization learn to ask for feedback, they begin to transform a feedback-averse environment into a more honest and open one, in turn improving performance throughout the organization.

Equally important, using the adaptive techniques we've mentioned can have a positive effect on executives' private lives. When they free themselves from knee-jerk behaviors in response to emotions, they often find that relationships with family and friends improve. Indeed, they sometimes discover that rather than fear feedback, they look forward to leveraging it.

Originally published in April 2003
Reprint R0304H

A New Game Plan for C Players

BETH AXELROD,

HELEN HANDFIELD-JONES, AND

ED MICHAELS

Executive Summary

IT'S A BIG DRIVER OF business success, but one that executives are loath to talk about: upgrading the talent pool by weeding out "C" players from management. These aren't the incompetent or unethical managers whom organizations dismiss without a backward glance; C performers deliver results that are acceptable–barely– but they fail to innovate or to inspire the people they lead.

The authors of *The War for Talent* have studied what it takes to upgrade an organization's talent pool. In this article, they explore the hidden costs of tolerating under-performance and acknowledge the reasons why executives may shy away from dealing decisively with C players. They recommend that organizations take an "iron hand in a velvet glove" approach to managing subpar performers. That is, companies should establish rigorous, disciplined processes for assessing and dealing with low-performing managers but still treat them with respect.

The authors outline three ironhanded steps. First, executives must *identify C players* by evaluating their talents and distributing employee performances along an assessment curve. Second, executives must *agree on explicit action plans* that articulate the improvements or changes that C performers must achieve within 6 to 12 months. And third, executives should *hold managers accountable* for carrying out the action plans. Without such discipline, procrastination, rationalization, and inaction will prevail.

The authors also emphasize the need for the "velvet glove." Executives must ensure that low performers are treated with dignity, so they should offer candid feedback, instructive coaching, and generous severance packages and outplacement support. The authors' approach isn't about being tough on people; it's about being relentlessly focused on performance.

ANY SEASONED EXECUTIVE would agree: The quality of a business's pool of managerial talent is a critical driver of its ongoing success. Yet very few organizations have a rigorous and consistent approach for managing that talent. Most companies struggle with even the fundamental task of assessing the relative performance of their people. And they are worse still at taking appropriate actions based on such assessments.

The shortcomings are particularly acute when it comes to managing underperformers. After all, a company's executives can experience real joy in recruiting, developing, and retaining "A" and "B" players. But dealing with "C" players is painful, and most avoid it.

Especially in these challenging economic times, companies need to have in place a strong cadre of leaders, and they need to make tough decisions about performance. Downsizing poses a particular challenge for many companies, because if it's not done well, the decisions about who stays and who goes can seem capricious. Indeed, it is difficult for employees to have confidence that decisions made in hard times are fully informed if the company does not systematically and rigorously assess its managers' performance in fertile times. Regularly removing the low-performing managers from an organization helps ensure its vitality—in good times and bad.

Over the past five years, we've been researching what it takes to build a pool of great managerial talent. We've surveyed 13,000 senior managers at 112 companies, studied 27 companies with reputations for top-tier talent, and consulted with more than 100 companies working to upgrade their talent pools. And we've observed that, as much as an organization's success depends on the careful management of A and B performers, it also depends on the pruning of C performers. Indeed, we have found that high-performing companies are 33% more likely to take deliberate action on C performers than average-performing companies are.

How do the high-performing businesses do it? What follows is an approach distilled from their most-effective practices—an approach we liken to an "iron hand in a velvet glove." That is, companies need to establish a rigorous, disciplined process for dealing with low-performing managers *and* they need to treat these people with great respect.

Barriers to Action

Before we discuss why dealing with C performers is so difficult, let's clarify what we mean by the term. We are not talking here about grossly incompetent or unethical managers; companies remove those individuals without hesitation. A company's C managers deliver acceptable results—just barely. They scrape by, and perhaps even progress incrementally, but they rarely create anything bold or innovative, and they don't inspire others. Note that the "C" refers not to the person but to the individual's performance in a given job. Some low-performing managers were A or B performers earlier in their careers—and may attain that level of performance again.

This begins to hint at why many companies undermanage C performers—at why, in fact, tolerating them has become an unspoken code of conduct. Even though managers would love to make room for more talented people, the act of confronting low performers is fraught with emotional, ideological, and practical barriers. According to our research, the primary reason executives don't act on C performers is understandably an emotional one: They are unwilling to move on people with whom they have worked for many years or people who have contributed to the company for so long. In many cases, a C performer has formed a friendship with his or her manager over time, and that emotional attachment can cloud the manager's objectivity. Even when there is little personal connection, the very human tendency to empathize with others comes into play. All of us have felt humiliation and loss, and few of us would wish it on others. Disciplining or firing someone is a painful and difficult process for everyone involved.

There are also ideological barriers to doing the hard work of managing C players. Some managers erroneously believe that all C performers can be developed into B or even A performers—and that the organization should invest in people indefinitely for this to happen. Other managers believe loyalty should be reciprocated, even when an individual's performance is lacking, or that it should be enough for someone to be trying his or her best. Les Wexner, CEO of clothing retailer The Limited, struggled with this issue of fairness. He asked himself, "Do I really want to identify a top, middle, and bottom tier of people reporting to me? Decisions around people's careers and responsibility to their families—those are the toughest." In the end, though, he found the other side of the equation more compelling: "If I don't make the tough decisions about the people who are preventing the enterprise from being successful, then I am putting at risk 175,000 people who are depending on that leadership."

Finally, practical barriers often prevent executives from taking action. Chief among them is the fear of litigation, fanned by the recent high-profile examples of companies being sued for racial, age, or gender discrimination after they implemented systems to identify low performers. Other practical barriers are the often onerous process of documenting underperformance and the fear that resentment and negativity will spread throughout the organization.

For all these reasons, most companies fail to deal with C performers. Indeed, just 19% of the thousands of senior managers we polled believe their companies remove low performers quickly and effectively. And while the managers surveyed surely sympathize with the plight of the C player, 96% of them said they would be delighted if their companies moved more aggressively on low performers. They can see that their organizations would prosper by doing so.

The True Cost of the C Player

The benefits of improving or removing low-performing managers are enormous, because their continued presence weakens the company in myriad ways. Obviously, they don't produce the results that A and B players do. In two companies we studied, the A managers grew profits, on average, 80% in one company and 130% in the other, while the C managers achieved no profit growth. This analysis points out what executives know intuitively: Holding on to underperforming managers pulls down a company's performance.

The economic argument for upgrading a company's leadership talent pool can be seen in several recent stories of dramatic improvement in corporate performance: The Limited reversed a plunge in its stock price to sustain a 23% annual total return to shareholders over a 20-year period. SunTrust Banks increased its growth rate from 4% to 10% within a year. And the high-tech company PerkinElmer tripled its market capitalization in three years. All three companies had adopted new business strategies and performance-improvement initiatives, but all three credit their successes in large part to their aggressive efforts to replace C performers with A and B performers.

Consider that every C performer fills a role and therefore blocks the advancement and development of other more talented people in an organization. At the same time, C performers usually aren't good role models, coaches, or mentors for others. Eighty percent of respondents in our survey said working for a low performer prevented them from learning, kept them from making greater contributions to the organization, and made them want to leave the company. Imagine, then, the collective impact on the talent pool and morale of a company if just 20 of its managers are underperformers and if each of them manages ten people.

In fact, keeping C performers in leadership positions lowers the bar for everyone—a clear danger for any company that wants to create a performance-focused culture. C performers hire other C performers, and their continued presence discourages the people around them, makes the company a less attractive place for highly talented people, and calls into question the judgment of senior leaders. As an executive at Arrow Electronics told us: "It's incredibly demoralizing for the rest of the team if you don't move poor performers out—and the leader looks blind and out of touch."

Clearly, tolerating the C performers in a company negatively affects the better performers in that company. But it also has a dispiriting and stressful effect on the C player, who is being kept in a position where he or she is incapable of performing well. Debra L. Dunn, vice president of strategy and corporate operations at Hewlett-Packard, put it this way: "I feel there is no greater disrespect you can do to a person than to let them hang out in a job where they are not respected by their peers, not viewed as successful, and probably losing their self-esteem. To do that under the guise of respect for people is, to me, ridiculous." (For more management tips, see "Talent Management Must-Haves" at the end of this article.)

An Iron Hand in a Velvet Glove

To build a strong talent pool, senior executives must regularly remove low performers from leadership positions.

They may want to take a different approach when it comes to low performers in other positions, such as front-line or unionized workers. But the imperative to do so in the senior managerial ranks is compelling.

To make this happen, companies need to apply an iron hand in a velvet glove. The phrase was coined by Napoleon Bonaparte to advocate firmness made more palatable and effective through courtesy and manners. We use it to mean a rigorous, disciplined process for dealing with low performers that also treats each individual with fairness and respect. Such an approach can counter the emotional, ideological, and practical barriers we cited earlier. Let's examine the application of the iron hand when it comes to dealing with C performers.

The iron hand is needed to overcome the procrastination, rationalization, and inaction that naturally occur around low performers. Companies need to establish a disciplined process that will *make* managers confront this difficult talent-management issue head-on. A disciplined approach will also bolster the integrity and credibility of the company's human resource processes in the eyes of *all* its employees. The discipline of managing C performers requires three steps: Executives must identify C players, they must agree on action plans for each, and they must hold managers accountable for carrying out the action plans.

IDENTIFY THE C PERFORMERS

In our survey of managers, only 16% of them strongly agreed that their companies knew who the high and low performers were in the senior ranks. To identify its low performers, a company needs clearly defined performance objectives and assessment criteria. Senior management must set distinct goals for all positions and measure individuals' performance against those goals. It must also articulate a set of leadership competencies—the skills and behaviors expected of all managers in the company. The CEO and division presidents have critical roles to play in setting these performance expectations, ensuring that the bar is set high enough and that it is consistent with the company's overall performance goals.

Executives then need to decide on a simple rating system to delineate performance levels—we've been talking about As, Bs, and Cs in this article, but many categorization schemes are possible. Some companies use a grid that plots performance on one axis and potential on the other to arrive at the ratings. SunTrust divides its 200 market managers into four categories: large-market growers, small-market growers, market maintainers, and strugglers.

The biggest challenge is getting managers to distribute people across these ratings buckets. Without a rigorous assessment process, the outcome of such a rating system is fairly predictable: Managers will rate most of their people as "outstanding" or "good." Thus, a company's senior leaders need to drive the organization toward an appropriate distribution of ratings. They should engage in robust discussions, even debates, about the performance improvements required by the company and the magnitude of the company's talent gap. With that information, they should set targets for the percentage of managers they expect to be designated as low performers.

There is no question that bell curves can be controversial, and they can be problematic—people often react negatively to the idea of strict adherence to performance quotas. But in organizations where identifying the highest and lowest performers is a widely accepted philosophy, the distribution approach needn't be so strict—managers understand the overall goal and can be trusted to come close enough to the distribution targets. In organizations where there is a great deal of resistance, the distribution might have to be more rigidly applied. Either way, the groups or units being reviewed must be large enough (at least 30 people) so that they reflect the typical range of performance levels in the company.

When pushing for clear differentiation between the highest performers and the lowest, a relative distribution of assessments is easier to accomplish than absolute assessments. That is, managers can usually assess whether Mary's performance is better than Peter's and worse than Nancy's even if they find it difficult to assess Mary's performance against the standard definition of a world-class manager. This relative approach also makes it clear that the objective of the process is to continuously upgrade the talent pool by improving or replacing the lowest performers, bringing in and growing more top performers, and raising everyone's game.

Assessing people and gaining insight into their strengths and weaknesses requires a rich base of information and multiple points of view. At the very least, three or more senior leaders should be included in the discussions about each person's performance. The best companies also use 360-degree feedback and self-assessments from individuals. Some leaders make a point of talking occasionally with the subordinates of the managers they will be assessing, asking them what's going well in the business and what isn't. Those informal conversations can reveal a lot about a manager's effectiveness.

AGREE ON EXPLICIT ACTION PLANS FOR EACH C PERFORMER

Once leaders have identified the lowest performers, they must articulate the specific actions that will be taken with each person in the coming six to 12 months. The action plan will depend on several considerations: Does the person want to improve? Does this person have some strong skills that are valuable to the company? Is this person in a job that is not suited to his or her skills? Has the person been in this job for too short a time to be able to judge his or her performance? Is there something in the individual's personal life that is sapping his or her energy at the moment? How much warning, help, and time has this person already been given? Then, one of three types of actions needs to be taken: Improve the C player's performance in this job to at least a B level, move the C player to a job that better matches his or her skills, or ask the C performer to leave the company.

Certainly, some C players can improve their performance substantially if given the direction and the developmental support to do so. For these people, the action plan should include the specific skills and results that must be demonstrated, clear timelines for accomplishing these improvements, and a description of the coaching support that will be provided. The message to the C performer should be unambiguous and encouraging. Leaders should be aware that some C players will improve, but others won't, and they should take care not to overinvest in the latter.

When development efforts are not successful, the company must either move C performers to more suitable jobs or ask them to leave the company. The Home Depot, SunTrust, and Intel are three companies that first try to

find their C performers roles in which they can contribute
more successfully. The Home Depot, for instance, will
even consider demotions: If a high-performing store manager is promoted to district manager and then fails in that
new role, the company sometimes offers to move that person back into a store manager role. Some people accept
the move; others prefer to leave. This approach allows the
person to stay with Home Depot and allows the company
to leverage the talent it already has. But the company also
runs the risk of placing people who have plateaued into
important managerial roles or of transferring problems
from one unit to another.

Companies that are unwilling to take that kind of risk,
such as GE, Arrow Electronics, and PerkinElmer, ask
those who have failed to improve in their job to leave the
company—except, of course, if there was an obvious mis-
match between the individual and the position. Bill
Conaty, senior vice president of human resources at GE,
explained the company's philosophy: "We are continually raising the performance bar for all our employees, so
the sooner in one's career that performance issues are
candidly addressed, the better for all concerned."

HOLD MANAGERS ACCOUNTABLE

Even the most explicit action plans will fail if managers
are not compelled to carry them out. Senior leaders
should hold their managers accountable for building
strong talent pools; carrying out the actions to improve or
remove C performers should be an explicit part of that.

First, in a very formal sense, the CEO and a senior
human resources executive should regularly follow up
with each of the unit leaders to check on implementation of any action plans and to help them overcome any

barriers. At SunTrust, for instance, this follow-up process includes a tracking system that reports on performance management at each of its 30 banks, allowing the CEO and division heads to see at a glance which banks are progressing well and which are not. The report shows the number of people who were identified in the last review process as C performers. It outlines the percentage of people who are in explicit improvement programs; who have adequately raised their performance; who were moved to more suitable positions; who have left the company; or who are still in place with no progress. Other companies formally check the progress of any talent action plans during their quarterly operational reviews.

SunTrust's leaders have instituted another practice that many more companies should imitate: They base a portion of their managers' compensation on how well they strengthen the talent pool. Up to 20% of the bank heads' bonuses depend on meeting the talent-building goals agreed to in their annual talent reviews, which often include specific objectives for managing low performers. This kind of formal accountability should be reinforced informally as well. In fact, frequent casual inquiries, advice, and encouragement from CEOs and division presidents may go furthest to signal the importance placed on effective talent management.

Of course, managers who are being asked to do something about their C performers should receive full support from their human resources and legal departments. But those groups sometimes hinder managers' efforts by advocating protection of employees and avoidance of all legal risk. Significant effort may be required to reorient these professionals toward teaching, counseling, and prodding line managers to exercise their talent-management responsibilities.

Companies can take steps to reduce the risk that their termination decisions will be challenged in court. Examples include early identification of performance issues in writing, with an opportunity for employees to address them; monitoring to assess whether certain groups inadvertently represent a disproportionate share of the proposed terminations; and offering severance in exchange for a release of legal claims.

All of these iron-hand steps—identifying C performers, developing action plans for them, and holding managers accountable for implementing the action plans—are best carried out through a talent review process, which the CEO and other senior leaders conduct at least once a year in each division. (For more information, see the exhibit "The Argument for Disciplined Talent Review.")

Ensuring Fairness and Respect

So far, we've been discussing the iron hand of discipline that companies need in order to identify and deal with C performers. But doing so in an insensitive way would be inhumane and could cause tremendous ill will between the organization and its employees. Companies must be very deliberate in ensuring that low performers—like all employees—are treated with dignity, respect, and care. That's where the "velvet glove" side of this directive comes into play. Senior management should note that candid feedback along the way, instructive coaching, and generous severance packages can help to ease the burden for underperformers, reduce managers' reluctance to identify low performers, and enhance trust in the way the company deals with its people generally.

DELIVER CANDID FEEDBACK ALONG THE WAY

Sugar-coating the truth about subpar performance is disrespectful and unfair; people need regular and candid feedback on how well they are doing and what they need to do to improve. Not telling people where they stand deprives them of the information they need to take responsibility for their development and to make informed decisions about their careers. Fully 89% percent of managers we surveyed said that candid, insightful feedback is very important to their development—yet only 39% said their companies do a good job of providing it.

All managers, no matter the level of their performance, have some distinctive strengths and some significant weaknesses that have been the basis for their past successes and failures. Telling C managers about their strengths affirms them and helps them find their way. Likewise, C performers benefit from unambiguous feedback about their weaknesses so they can overcome them. Most managers need to get a lot better at delivering both kinds of honest, constructive feedback. This feedback should be delivered in writing as part of an annual performance review and informally throughout the year. Termination for low performance should never come as a surprise.

OFFER INSTRUCTIVE COACHING TO HELP C PLAYERS IMPROVE

Telling people to improve without providing the requisite coaching and support is unhelpful; the individual may feel like he or she is being set up to be fired. C performers need

The Argument for Disciplined Talent Review

We surveyed thousands of managers in a broad range of companies about their approaches to talent review and succession planning. Consistently, we found that managers from high-performing companies applied more attention, discipline, and energy to identifying and taking action on A, B, and C players than their lower-performing counterparts did. The charts below show the percentage of corporate officers who strongly agree that their companies' review processes demonstrate the following characteristics:

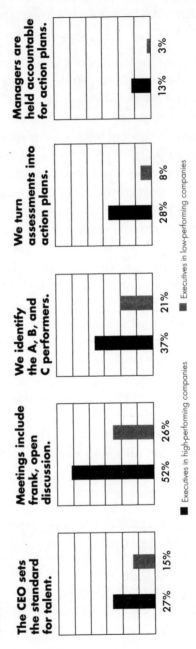

The CEO sets the standard for talent.

27%
15%

Meetings include frank, open discussion.

52%
26%

We identify the A, B, and C performers.

37%
21%

We turn assessments into action plans.

28%
8%

Managers are held accountable for action plans.

13%
3%

■ Executives in high-performing companies   ■ Executives in low-performing companies

Unfortunately, the traditonal approach to succession planning often falls short . . .

In too many companies, the standard for leadership is vague. Without clearly articulated assessment criteria, the caliber of managerial talent begins to erode and is inconsistent from one unit to another.

In a typical talent review meeting, one manager presents each assessment while the rest listen with polite, senatorial courtesy. A half day of presentations occurs at corporate centers. Instead, a full day of intense discussions should take place at each division.

Most companies focus on identifying successors, not on assessing incumbents. They don't calibrate their assessments of managers. And everyone is rated in shades of gray.

Most companies don't articulate what actions will be taken regarding an individual's performance. They don't decide what will be done in the coming year to advance, develop, reward, demote, or replace each person.

Most companies have no disciplined process for ensuring that managers implement the plans discussed during the talent review. Nor are most managers measured on how well they have upgraded their talent pools.

specific guidance on how to do things differently in order to make a significant change in their performance.

One effective practice uncovered by our research was the formal "corrective action plan" used at Arrow Electronics. This program is more constructive than punitive; it specifies what the individual must do to improve within a defined period of time (up to six months), and it requires the supervisor to provide frequent coaching to help the person achieve these new behaviors. If performance has not sufficiently improved at the end of that period, the person is asked to leave—but Arrow reports that about half the people who go through the corrective-action process succeed and sustain an acceptable level of performance consistently thereafter.

GIVE THE C PERFORMER GENEROUS SEPARATION SUPPORT

When it finally comes down to firing someone for subpar performance, providing the individual with generous support goes a long way toward lessening any hardships, anger, and legal risks. Every company should have regular policies and procedures for severance payments. They should also have the flexibility to go beyond standard compensation packages when confronted by particularly difficult cases. Some companies deliberately provide very generous severance as a way to make the whole experience more palatable. But the support should go well beyond money. It should include outplacement services to help the person find a new job, as well as counsel and job leads from managers in the company. An office and secretarial support can also make the search process more manageable.

Leaders may also need to help the C performer through the emotional turmoil of being terminated. Chuck

Okosky, formerly vice president of executive development at GE, recalls one senior manager he helped through the exit process: "I spent several hours with him immediately after his boss fired him. He shouted, cried, and talked about his family. It was a way for him to off-load his anger and get through the negative emotion as quickly as possible." Over the next few months, Okosky introduced the manager to outplacement consultants and counseled him on the types of jobs he might consider pursuing.

All too often, the leader avoids contact with the C performer after firing him or her. But the leader and HR executives have a responsibility to help this person exit the company with dignity. They have to transcend their own discomfort and support the individual through this difficult transition. For information on how to treat A and B performers fairly, see "What About A and B Performers?" at the end of this article.

Start at the Top

Recently, a *BusinessWeek* columnist asked GE's Jack Welch to sum up why he was so successful. "My main job was developing talent," he explained. "I was a gardener providing water and other nourishment to our top 750 people." But Welch also hastened to add, "Of course, I had to pull out some weeds, too."

This comment underscores the importance of dealing with low performers. It also emphasizes that upgrading the talent pool must start with commitment from the top. A recent study of unsuccessful CEOs underscores this point: It suggested that the most common reason for the CEOs' failure was that they didn't remove the low performers from among their own direct reports. As the authors of the study, Geoffrey Colvin and Ram Charan, reported in *Fortune*: "The failure is one of emotional strength."

Any company embarking on a talent upgrade would do well to address its senior-most management ranks first—its top 50 to 150 managers. With such a small group, the CEO and other senior leaders can be directly involved and can ensure the integrity of the process. It also means that when the process is subsequently pushed down to the next 200 to 350 managers, the executives conducting the talent review will have experienced the process and will be better equipped to implement it. Companies should not push the talent review process beyond the top few hundred people until it's working very well at that level; the required skills and values take time to build, and legal and morale risks grow with the size of the group affected.

Overcoming the natural tendency to turn a blind eye to underperforming managers starts with the dual recognition that building a strong talent pool is critical to driving the company's performance and that effectively managing low performers is essential to doing that. Indeed, regularly improving or removing C performers is good for the individuals involved, good for the people around them, and good for the company.

Decisively dealing with C performers isn't about a one-time housecleaning or downsizing. It's about constantly holding the company's performance bar high and making sure that the company's leaders live up to that standard. Nor is it about being tough on people; it's about being relentlessly focused on performance.

Talent Management Must-Haves

THE APPROACH TO managing C players that we're discussing in this article is just one piece of an overall program for managing talent effectively. In order to cultivate managerial talent at all levels of the company, leaders should adhere to the following five imperatives, which distinguish high-performing companies from average ones. The imperatives are the subject of our book, *The War for Talent.*

1. Embrace a talent mind-set, and make talent management a critical part of every manager's job.

2. Create a winning "employee value proposition" that provides a compelling reason for a highly talented person to join and stay with your company.

3. Rebuild your recruiting strategies to inject talent at all levels, from many sources, and to respond to the ebbs and flows in the talent market.

4. Weave development into the organization by deliberately using stretch jobs, candid feedback, coaching, and mentoring to grow every manager's talents.

5. Differentiate the performance of your people, and affirm their unique contributions to the organization.

The fifth imperative includes and goes beyond dealing explicitly with low performers. It addresses the broader need to differentiate the strong players from the weak players in a company's entire talent pool, and it implies the need to invest in and grow A and B performers.

What About A and B Performers?

ACTING ON C PERFORMERS IS only part of managing a talent pool effectively; companies need to be just as deliberate in managing A and B performers.

The A performers create significant value for their companies directly and through their leadership of others. The objectives with A performers are to accelerate their development and to do everything you can to retain them.

The B performers are the solidly contributing majority of a company's managerial force. Collectively, they are critical to the success of the business. They should be developed and affirmed so they realize more of their potential and feel valued for their unique contributions.

Ultimately, A and B performers require the same types of developmental actions, including the following:

- Accelerate their professional development through a steady stream of challenging job assignments.

- Encourage their involvement in tasks outside their jobs so they are connected to a broader network and build a stronger sense of belonging.

- Assign mentors to nurture their development and to help retain them.

- Offer candid feedback about their weaknesses, and praise them for their distinctive strengths.

- Recognize and reward their contributions.

One challenge for executives is determining how to allocate a company's scarce resources among the A and B performers. High-quality coaching, seasoned mentors, generous compensation, promotions, and highly visible roles are often in short supply, so they need to be invested in those people with the highest performance and potential.

Originally published in January 2002
Reprint R0201G

Getting 360-Degree Feedback Right

MAURY A. PEIPERL

Executive Summary

OVER THE PAST DECADE, 360-degree feedback has revolutionized performance management. But one of its components—peer appraisal—consistently stymies executives and can exacerbate bureaucracy, heighten political tensions, and consume lots of time.

For ten years, Maury Peiperl has studied 360-degree feedback and has asked: under what circumstances does peer appraisal improve performance? Why does peer appraisal sometimes work well and sometimes fail? And how can executives make these programs less anxiety provoking for participants and more productive for organizations? Peiperl discusses four paradoxes inherent to peer appraisal:

- In the Paradox of Roles, colleagues juggle being both peer and judge.

- The Paradox of Group Performance navigates between assessing individual feedback and the reality that much of today's work is done by groups.

- The Measurement Paradox arises because simple, straightforward rating systems would seem to generate the most useful appraisals—but they don't. Customized, qualitative feedback, though more difficult and time consuming to generate, is more helpful in improving performance.

- During evaluations, most people focus almost exclusively on reward outcomes and ignore the constructive feedback generated by peer appraisal. Ironically, it is precisely this overlooked feedback that helps improve performance—thus, the Paradox of Rewards.

These paradoxes do not have neat solutions, but managers who understand them can better use peer appraisal to improve their organizations.

I F A SINGLE E-MAIL CAN send the pulse racing, it's the one from human resources announcing that it's time for another round of 360-degree feedback. In and of itself, this type of appraisal isn't bad. Indeed, many business-people would argue that over the past decade, it has revolutionized performance management—for the better. But one aspect of 360-degree feedback consistently stymies executives: peer appraisal. More times than not, it exacerbates bureaucracy, heightens political tensions, and consumes enormous numbers of hours. No wonder so many executives wonder if peer appraisal is worth the effort.

I would argue that it is. Peer appraisal, when conducted effectively, can bolster the overall impact of 360-

degree feedback and is as important as feedback from superiors and subordinates. Yet the question remains: can peer appraisal take place without negative side effects? The answer is yes—if executives understand and manage around four inherent paradoxes.

For the past ten years, my research has focused on the theory behind, and practice of, 360-degree feedback. Most recently, I studied its implementation at 17 companies varying in size—from start-ups of a few dozen people to *Fortune* 500 firms—and industry—from high-tech manufacturing to professional services firms. I was looking for answers to several questions. Under what circumstances does peer appraisal improve performance? Why does peer appraisal work well in some cases and fail miserably in others? And finally, how can executives fashion peer appraisal programs to be less anxiety provoking and more productive for the organization?

My research produced a discomforting conclusion: peer appraisal is difficult because it has to be. Four inescapable paradoxes are embedded in the process:

- *The Paradox of Roles:* You cannot be both a peer and a judge.

- *The Paradox of Group Performance:* Focusing on individuals puts the entire group at risk.

- *The Measurement Paradox:* The easier feedback is to gather, the harder it is to apply.

- *The Paradox of Rewards:* When peer appraisal counts the most, it helps the least.

Performance management isn't easy under any circumstances. But a certain clarity exists in the traditional form of performance review, when a boss evaluates a subordinate. The novelty and ambiguity of peer appraisal, on the other hand, give rise to its paradoxes. Fortunately, managers can, with some forward thinking and a deeper understanding of their dynamics, ease the discomfort. Let's consider each paradox in detail.

The Paradox of Roles

Peer appraisal begins with a simple premise: the people best suited to judge the performance of others are those who work most closely with them. In flatter organizations with looser hierarchies, bosses may no longer have all the information they need to appraise subordinates. But it doesn't necessarily follow that peers will eagerly step into the breach. They may tend to give fairly conservative feedback rather than risk straining relationships with colleagues by saying things that could be perceived negatively. Consequently, the feedback gathered from peers may be distorted, overly positive, and, in the end, unhelpful to managers and recipients.

In more than one team I studied, participants in peer appraisal routinely gave all their colleagues the highest ratings on all dimensions. When I questioned this practice, the responses revealed just how perplexing and risky, both personally and professionally, evaluating peers can be. Some people feared that providing negative feedback would damage relationships and ultimately hurt their own careers and those of their friends and colleagues. Others resisted because they preferred to give feedback informally rather than making it a matter of record. Still other employees resented peer appraisal's playing a part in a performance system that resulted in promotions for some and criticism and even punishment for others—thereby, they believed, compromising the egalitarian and supportive work environments they had tried to cultivate.

When the Paradox of Roles is at play, people are torn between being supportive colleagues or hard-nosed judges. Their natural inclination is to offer counsel and encouragement, and yet they've been asked to pass judgment on a colleague's performance. Unless this conflict is addressed early on, peer appraisal will go nowhere fast—and cause stress and resentment along the way.

The Paradox of Group Performance

Most peer appraisal programs can't reveal what makes a great group tick. Even though such evaluations are intended to gain insights into the workings of teams or groups, peer appraisal programs usually still target individual performance. In most cases, however, a focus on individuals doesn't address how most important work is done these days—that is, through flexible, project-based teams. Moreover, successful groups resent it when management tries to shift their focus or asks them to compare members with one another; in the extreme, peer appraisal may even harm close-knit and successful groups.

In one high-performing group I studied—the venture capital arm of a well-known bank—peer appraisal was roundly viewed as an annoyance of questionable utility. This group was utterly dismissive of the bank's appraisal system, even though the program was well constructed, aggressively backed by top management, and successful in other areas of the bank. The members considered themselves a highly independent group and believed they were already fully aware of their performance, both individually and in project teams. To their way of thinking, they had already created a collegial and cohesive environment that delivered extraordinary results for the company, so why couldn't the bank just leave them alone? The group's finely honed balance of status and responsibilities was threatened by the prospect of individual peer appraisals. Although they halfheartedly participated in one round of 360-degree feedback, over time they simply stopped completing the evaluation forms, thus registering their contempt for (and possibly their fear of) the program.

Low-performing groups also often greet peer appraisal unenthusiastically. At a professional services firm, I met with the partners in charge of a practice that had suffered a long, slow decline in profitability. They saw peer appraisal as a veiled attempt by the rest of the organization to assess blame. As a form of passive protest, this group provided few comments when evaluating one another, and when pressed to discuss results, they resisted. So great was the threat implied by peer appraisal that eventually they refused outright to discuss any feedback they had received, and the process shut down altogether. Their worries about their own failure and the company's motivations became self-fulfilling: as their willingness to discuss results diminished, so did the practice's performance.

As these cases suggest, when peer appraisal ignores group dynamics and work realities, it delivers counterproductive results. If most work is done in groups, focusing on individuals can compromise the group's performance or make a weak team's performance even worse. Rather than cultivating a sense of shared ownership and responsibility, the process can breed deep cynicism, suspicion, and an "us-against-them" mentality—the exact opposite of the values most companies espouse.

The Measurement Paradox

It seems logical that simple, objective, straightforward rating systems should generate the most useful appraisals. Number or letter grades make it easier for managers to gather, aggregate, and compare ratings across individuals and groups, and they often just *seem* like the right way to proceed (after all, most of us have been getting report cards since kindergarten). But ratings by themselves don't yield the detailed, qualitative comments and insights that can help a colleague improve performance. In fact, the simpler the measures and the fewer dimensions on which an individual is measured, the less useful the evaluation.

One media company I observed was especially proud of its performance measurement program, which involved elaborate rounds of evaluations by peers and bosses. The process culminated in a letter grade for every individual, which was then linked to group, division, and, ultimately, corporate results. Top executives were pleased with this approach because of the links it recognized within and between groups. However, many of the employees expressed frustration, not only because the process required an excessive amount of paperwork but also because the system lacked a mechanism for giving or getting detailed feedback beyond a letter grade. Employees frequently reported satisfaction with their ratings, but they complained that they lacked a clear sense of what they had done to deserve their grades and, more important, what they were doing wrong and needed to address in order to progress in their careers.

"It's comforting to know I'm an A-plus," one person reported, "but where do I go from here?"

Simple ratings are not always bad, but most of the time they are not enough. Of course, qualitative feedback is more difficult and time-consuming to generate and is not as easily compared and aggregated. It can pose problems of interpretation when comments are personal or highly idiosyncratic (such as, "She is the class of the outfit."). But without specific comments, recipients are left with no information to act on and with little sense of what might help them get better at their jobs.

The Paradox of Rewards

Most people are keenly attuned to peer appraisal when it affects salary reviews and promotions. In the short term, employees may take steps to improve performance (a perpetual latecomer may start showing up on time). But most people focus virtually all their attention on reward outcomes ("Am I going to get a raise or not?"), ignoring the more constructive feedback that peer appraisal generates. Ironically, it is precisely this overlooked feedback that could help to improve performance. Most people don't deliberately ignore peer appraisal feedback, but even the most confident and successful find it hard to interpret objectively when it is part of the formal reward system. In these instances, peer appraisal poses a threat to feelings of self-worth—not to mention net worth.

Is the solution, then, to take rewards out of the equation? My research suggests that the answer is not nearly so straightforward. Consider this contradiction: in many organizations I surveyed, raters expressed reservations about providing critical feedback when they knew it would directly influence another's salary. One participant put it, "You could destroy somebody and not even know it." But when I queried recipients of peer appraisal, many reported that they weren't interested in feedback unless it "had teeth." If the results were seen as being for "HR purposes," not "business purposes," recipients were less inclined to take the process seriously; if peer feedback didn't have an impact on rewards, it often wasn't used.

With the Paradox of Rewards, managers find themselves in a catch-22. When rewards are on the line, peer appraisal may generate a lot of activity but usually delivers only short-term improvements in performance from feedback that may be conservative or incomplete. When not tied to rewards, feedback is likely to be more comprehensive (and thus potentially useful) but is not seen as important by recipients, who may delay in addressing it or ignore it altogether.

Managing Through the Paradoxes

As might be expected, these paradoxes do not have neat solutions. They are best seen not as obstacles to be overcome but as features of the appraisal landscape to be managed around or even through. The nature of a paradox isn't easily changed, but the way it is viewed can be. Indeed, one of the most significant findings from my research is the pivotal role that managers play in successful peer appraisal. My field notebooks are full of comments from participants about their managers—some commending bosses for active participation, and others condemning behavior that undermined the process. In too many organizations, I've seen peer appraisal programs sabotaged by managers who let it be known through off-hand comments or their own lack of participation that peer appraisal might be well and good for everyone else, but not for them. The best managers, on the other hand, act as constructive critics, role models, and willing participants. (See "Managing the 'Peer' in Peer Appraisal" at the end of this article.)

My findings also suggest that managers and organizations don't spend enough time asking themselves and conveying to employees why peer appraisal is being used. The potential benefits may seem obvious at first, but when the purpose and the scope of peer appraisal are not made explicit, conflict soon takes over.

PURPOSE

In most cases, the purpose of peer appraisal is to provide timely and useful feedback to help individuals improve their performance. Detailed, qualitative feedback from peers accompanied by coaching and supportive counseling from a manager are essential. If participants understand the reasons for soliciting this kind of feedback, some of the tension of the Measurement Paradox can be overcome. If, however, the purpose of peer appraisal is simply to check that things are going smoothly and to head off major conflicts, a quick and dirty evaluation using only a few numbers will suffice. In one small organization that used only number ratings, the CEO regularly reviewed all feedback summaries; when any two employees' ratings of each other were unusually negative, he brought them together and helped them address their differences. This practice worked because its purpose was explicit—to catch conflicts before they turned into full-blown crises—and because the CEO's visibility actively mitigated the effects of the Measurement Paradox.

Occasionally, peer appraisal is used to improve ties between groups. In these cases, managers should focus the appraisal effort on the entire group rather than on particular members. When groups themselves realize the need for improved links, the effects of the Paradox of Group Performance may be stemmed. In one situation I witnessed, the sales and operations groups in a large financial services firm were not cooperating, and customer complaints were piling up. The manager invited members of each group to provide anonymous feedback to people in the other group. At first, the feedback was terse and critical, but when each group saw that the company was using the feedback not to reward or punish individuals but to highlight the problems between the two groups, the feedback became more extensive and constructive. Eventually, peer evaluation became a regular channel of communication to identify and resolve conflicts between these groups. In this example, peer appraisal succeeded because it first addressed the real-world conflicts that had led to unmet customer demands; only when participants became accustomed to the process was it folded into the formal reward system, thus decreasing the effects of the Paradox of Rewards.

I have also seen peer appraisal programs introduced as part of larger empowerment programs aimed at distributing authority and responsibility more broadly throughout an organization. In one manufacturing company I studied, a group of factory workers designed its own peer evaluation process. The group already performed multiple roles and functions on the factory floor and took responsibility for hiring, training, and quality control, so it also made sense for the members to take charge of evaluating one another's work. Instead of seeing conflict in the new roles, group members saw peer appraisal as a continuation of the other responsibilities they had assumed. The Paradox of Roles was barely evident.

SCOPE

Managers also need to be selective about how broadly peer appraisal, and 360-degree programs in general, are used. In the name of inclusion, many organizations feel compelled to roll out these programs everywhere. But democracy is overrated, at least when it comes to peer appraisal. One large financial services firm I studied had great success in solving business process issues across several front-office groups through the judicious use of peer evaluation. The process resulted in widely celebrated improvements and better relations between the front-office groups, so much so that other groups in the company wanted to join in. But when the firm introduced the same program to the additional thousand-plus employees, the program collapsed under its own weight. By trying to provide substantial, but in many cases unnecessary, feedback to all, the company compromised its ability to function.

In choosing rating criteria for peer appraisal, it's also important to remember that all jobs are not the same. A customized evaluation takes longer to develop, but as the Measurement Paradox suggests, such an investment of time and effort is crucial because inappropriate or narrowly defined criteria are difficult for peer evaluators to use and even harder for recipients to apply. Moreover, if participants detect that the system is unlikely to improve their performance or rewards, they are even less likely to actively engage in the process with their peers, as the Paradox of Rewards illustrates.

The Paradox of Group Performance will be less of an issue when the right balance is achieved between evaluating the contributions of individuals and acknowledging the interdependencies and connections within groups and across boundaries. Most organizations are notoriously bad at this, often touting teamwork and group performance while assiduously rewarding only individual outcomes. But in a few groups I studied, where the overall size of the bonus pool, for example, depended on everyone's ability to work together, the tension between individual contributions and group outcomes was kept in check. Practices like this not only diminished the effects of the Paradox of Group Performance but also dampened the effects of the Paradox of Rewards, in part because peer appraisal, while tied to rewards, was only one criterion used to decide them. This middle-ground approach to the Paradox of Rewards can work well when participants trust the integrity of the reward determination process.

In the ten years I have spent observing 360-degree feedback, I have seen a number of organizations gradually develop enough trust and confidence to make the most of peer appraisal without incurring dysfunctional consequences. These organizations recognize that 360-degree feedback systems, and peer appraisal programs in particular, are always works in progress—subject to vulnerabilities, requiring sensitivity to hidden conflicts as much as to tangible results, but nevertheless responsive to thoughtful design and purposeful change. Companies that have success with these programs tend to be open to learning and willing to experiment. They are led by executives who are direct about the expected benefits as well as the challenges and who actively demonstrate support for the process. By laying themselves open to praise and criticism from all directions and inviting others to do the same, they guide their organizations to new capacities for continuous improvement.

Managing the "Peer" in Peer Appraisal

MOST MANAGERS ARE STILL not accustomed to giving in-depth, constructive feedback. But by learning how to give feedback better—constructively, specifically, and in a timely manner—and by encouraging others to follow suit, managers themselves become the key ingredient in the peer appraisal process.

Go public with your support.

Let it be known that you value peer appraisal, and explicitly describe the benefit you and others have gained as a result of your own participation.

Be a counselor and role model.

Meet with subordinates to help them understand the assessments they receive, and engage them in discussions of the appraisals and their interpretation—without letting your own opinions dominate. Demystify the process by being open to feedback and self-improvement and by asking for input from others, including subordinates and peers.

Provide training early and often.

Allocate time and resources to help raters and recipients practice giving and receiving feedback. This is best accomplished in small groups and small doses, rather than through big, formal training programs.

Put substance before rankings.

Pay attention to and publicize results brought about through the feedback system, such as stronger links between departments, cost-saving innovations, and better information flows. Don't emphasize the success of individuals with high feedback numbers because then people may view 360-degree feedback as a popularity contest rather than a tool for improvement.

Let people know when they're not doing peer appraisal well.

Better yet, let their peers tell them. Set high expectations of your own peers and hold them to it. These skills only improve with practice, so scheduling time now and then to role-play with colleagues or trainers is worthwhile.

Originally published in January 2001
Reprint R0101K

Taking Time Seriously in Evaluating Jobs

ELLIOTT JAQUES

Executive Summary

THE FIRST QUESTION IS FAIRLY SIMPLE: How can we determine that one job is bigger or more weighty than another? If we use a usual job evaluation procedure, we may end up with a reasonable rating for two jobs in the same company, the same office, the same location, at the same time. But most evaluation procedures cannot straddle different companies, locations, and occupants of jobs. Searching for another approach, the author of this article, a well-known sociologist and psychoanalyst, shows how jobs can be evaluated based on the measurement of the maximum time allowed to complete the longest tasks. This measure is the time span of discretion, and it can be correlated not only with people's sense of fair pay in a job but also with a universal underlying structure of managerial organizations. What started as the author's quest for an answer to a seemingly simple question leads him and the reader to a universal structure of organizations and a hypothesis about the very nature of human capability at work.

IN APPRAISING PERFORMANCE, designing pay systems, and in organizing and planning work, managers make assessments about the size and importance of jobs. Whether the assessments are accurate deeply affects how well the organization runs. But what do we mean when we say that one job is bigger than another? Bigger in what sense?

One way or another, we would all agree that a chief executive officer's job is bigger than a copy typist's or a semiskilled manual worker's in the same company. We might say that it carries more or a wider span of responsibility, calls for more initiative, or (perhaps) requires more training. Or we might say that the chief executive officer is accountable for their work, while the reverse does not hold.

If we compare the CEO's role with that of his or her production director or sales manager, however, it becomes more difficult to state whether or why his or her role is bigger. We might still say that because he or she is the top manager the job must inevitably be bigger than any subordinate jobs. But we should still be hard put to say how much bigger.

And, most difficult of all, the moment we try to compare any two jobs in different parts of the organization we are in trouble. How do we compare, for example, an accountant with a production engineer, with a salesman, with a shop foreman, with a production controller, with a patent officer, with a research program manager, with a designer? Which is biggest and which is smallest?

Which is worth more and which less? Which should have higher status and which less? And how do we explain the differences to people actually in the jobs?

One of the things that all jobs have in common is time. Any experienced manager, whatever his or her job, takes the great importance of time for granted. Things have to be done on time, planning is done about time, and organizing is done to achieve things in time. Sales efforts have to mesh with production capacity and programs; invoices and accounts have to be sent out and payments received on schedule; raw materials and other supplies have to be ordered and deliveries ensured to connect with production schedules; wages and salaries have to be made out and paid at a precise hour; research investigations have to be completed on time or research budgets and programs will go haywire; and so on for every function in the organization.

In short, one way of looking at a functioning management system is as a complex and delicately balanced time machine. Within this time machine, everyone carries out tasks or assignments linked to one another in time. One important aspect of the task of managers, therefore, is to set target completion times for getting jobs done, and in such a way that everything meshes together. It is what they get paid for.

Because of its universality, I propose to use the peculiar significance of time in management as a basis for measuring the size of a job. Using a time-based measure, a manager can objectively determine the size of responsibility in any job, at any level, at any time. With this objective yardstick it becomes possible to compare any two jobs—in the same company or in different companies—and to compare any job with itself at different times to discover whether it has changed in size or responsibility.

Using the measure, which I call the time span of discretion, a manager can move toward solving two major managerial problems:

1. How to design a systematic payment structure, right across the board.

2. How to design a systematic and flexible organization structure with full-blooded managerial roles.

Let us begin by reviewing some problems of job evaluation that will be familiar to most managers.

Limits of Job Evaluation

How to determine the size of a job or compare its size with another is, of course, the problem that job evaluation procedures are supposed to resolve. Because job evaluation procedures are cumbersome, imprecise, and rigid they are unable to cope satisfactorily with change. And they do not directly and explicitly reflect the things people are expected to do in their jobs, the things they are employed and paid to get done.

It will be useful to consider some of the common difficulties inherent in the three main job evaluation procedures—points rating, factor comparison, and paired comparison—as currently practiced.

1. BASED ON JUDGMENT

All these job evaluation procedures require that a group of people, usually the person in the job being evaluated, a personnel specialist, a consultant, and perhaps a staff or union representative, plus others, agrees on all aspects of the job. This working group begins by describing the responsibilities in the job. Unfortunately, these people usually describe the responsibilities in terms of general activities such as typing letters, routine review of invoices, placing orders, seeing customers, achieving production targets, or numbers of subordinates, and so on. The description, however, never covers specific letters to be typed, particular invoices, the processing of any specific orders, or getting a particular customer to make a particular purchase.

Using these general descriptions of general responsibilities as the basis of intuitive judgments, each member of the evaluation committee rates each job. These intuitive ratings may be of particular criteria such as reasoning power, accountability, versatility, skill, length of training, or of general specifications covering the job as a whole. The group then tries to agree about the job by giving it a point rating. To do this, the group compares it to other jobs by examining various factors, such as amount of judgment required, or length of training, or amount of know-how, or by ranking the jobs themselves.

Of course, whatever results from this rests on the individual judgments of the group. If these judgments are good, then good results ensue; but serious difficulties can arise. It is not possible to know how good one group member's judgment is compared with another's. Hunches and intuitions cannot be measured by an objective yardstick when differences of opinion arise and compromises have to be arranged.

2. NONCOMPARABLE DATA

Another difficulty with job evaluation procedures is that data from two companies are not comparable. Nor is it possible to compare widely disparate types of jobs with any accuracy. The judgments of the different evaluation committees may differ, without anyone knowing by how much. Ultimately, the committees decide the comparative levels by negotiating and bargaining.

Similarly, it is not easy, and usually not possible, to compare jobs over a period of time. During one, two, or five years, people on a rating committee or rating methods may have changed. Each time the procedure must start again.

3. STRUCTURALLY INCONSISTENT SYSTEMS

Finally, job evaluation procedures are not related inherently to any particular compensation system. The job evaluation ratings and a particular organization structure may and often do in fact work against each other.

Time Span of Discretion

In putting forward a time-based method of job measurement, I will try to show that it overcomes these shortcomings in job evaluation. Time is objective; it applies equally to all jobs at all levels, in all companies, in all countries. A job's time span changes only as the level of the work changes. Just as we expect that all two-foot sticks will be the same length wherever they are (on earth, that is), so we can expect that all jobs with a two-month time span will have the same weight of responsibility whoever holds them.

The essence of time-span measurement is that it is based not on vague general statements about "responsibilities" but on specific and concrete statements of real tasks that a real manager expects his real subordinate to carry out.

Actual tasks or assignments are specific and concrete. There is nothing vague about them. With some thought, any manager ought to be able to detail the assignments he expects his subordinates to carry out such as:

- Inducting a new subordinate in 4 months.

- Establishing a new marketing outlet in 2 years.

- Typing a small handbook in 10 days.

- Completing the installation of a new process in 15 months.

- Working up a contract with a new customer in 6 months.

- Ordering and planning for delivery of a new machine tool in 9 months.

- Getting the necessary information and preparing a planning memorandum and recommendation in 15 months.

When I say that a manager expects a subordinate to be carrying out a task, I do not necessarily mean that the manager himself has assigned it. He may have initiated it, or the subordinate may have initiated it, or someone else might have asked the subordinate to do it. But whatever the case, a framework or a practice, stated or unstated, allows the subordinate to judge what his manager would expect and to get on with it.

I will go into some detailed examples of tasks and time-span measurement in the next section. But first I want to note a few important points:

1. EVERY CONCRETE TASK THAT SOMEONE IS REQUIRED TO DO HAS A TARGET COMPLETION TIME

(I emphasize that I am referring to specific tasks, such as "carry out this supervisory training program during the next 6 months," and not to general statements of responsibilities, such as "keep your subordinates sufficiently well trained.") A target completion time may have been explicitly set, or, just as often, it may be implied. But even if it is implicit, a manager ought to be able, if asked, to state what the target completion time is. This idea may not make immediate sense but it is a simple fact of the reality of management that it must be true. If tasks did not have completion times, no manager could control the working activity of his subordinates, nor would he have even a vague sense whether a specific employee was performing well. The work system would become uncoordinated and would fail as a system.

2. THE HIGHER A PERSON GOES IN AN EXECUTIVE SYSTEM, THE LONGER IS THE TIME FRAMEWORK WITHIN WHICH HE OR SHE WORKS

Everyone usually has many tasks that need to get done within hours or days. But many people also have tasks in their total mix of work that are targeted for completion in weeks, months, or years. The higher one goes in an organization, the more the time scale of the longer tasks increases. A person may still have many very short daily tasks but the longest tasks get longer and longer as he works his way to the top.

And now I come to my main point:

3. A JOB'S SIZE CAN BE DIRECTLY AND SIMPLY MEASURED BY COMPLETION TIMES TARGETED FOR THE LONGEST TASKS THAT ARE REQUIRED TO BE CARRIED OUT IN THAT ROLE, NAMELY, THE TIME SPAN OF DISCRETION

A number of striking findings led me to this conclusion about the significance of the time span of discretion:

- The time span of discretion coincides very closely with people's judgments about fair pay for the work involved. Thus the same time span will result in the same statement of fair pay regardless of the actual occupation or pay.

- The time span at which successive levels emerge in all managerial hierarchies is remarkably consistent. New levels emerge at 3 months, 1 year, 2 years, 5 years, 10 years, and longer.

- When the time span of a person's role decreases, he feels his weight of responsibility growing lighter; and when it increases, he feels the weight growing heavier.

Before I go into these findings in more detail, let us look at just how the time span of discretion is measured.[1]

Making a Time-Span Measurement

In describing the actual measurement of a job, I will deal only with multiple-task roles; that is to say, roles in which a person has several or many tasks at any given time and must decide on his priorities. Nearly all managerial, professional, and technical roles are of this type. They contrast with single-task roles in which a person has only one task at a time that he finishes before going on to the next. Most manual and clerical jobs are of this latter kind. The principles of time-span measurement apply to both, though the procedures vary slightly.

The first thing to do when making a measure is to talk with the *manager* of the role to be measured. The manager, in the final analysis, *decides* what the target completion times for his subordinates will be. Time spans are objective facts that the managers decide.

True, in determining these target times, a manager may have all sorts of things in mind. Different managers might set different times. And the same manager might set different times for two different subordinates. But once the manager does decide, these decisions become facts that have objective reality for his subordinate. They set the goals of the subordinate's work.

In doing a time-span measurement for the first time, it helps first to try it out on a friend who is a manager and whose work you know something about. Ask him or her one simple question: "Give me examples of tasks which you expect your subordinate to carry out that have the longest forward target completion. What is it you expect him to do, and by when do you require it to be done?"

If it is difficult to get a target completion time, use successive approximation. Ask: "Do you expect it to be completed within, say, 20 years?" Your friend will undoubtedly expostulate, and say "no." Then ask: "Do you expect it to be completed within a day?" Your friend will again expostulate, and say "not possible." He or she will then probably become a little more clear and tell you that it is closer to 1 year, or 6 months, or 2 years, or whatever, that he or she has in mind. You can help him or her to home more precisely on the actual *maximum* time he or she would allow.

Let me illustrate by giving examples of some longest tasks that I have found in jobs of various types:

- Against an anticipated gross change in technology, a CEO of a large corporation employing 40,000 people had to ensure progress in the development of entirely new products and market outlets within 15 years.

- A CEO of a smaller company had 7 years to arrange the design and development of a new manufacturing technology in the company's two factories.

- An owner-manager of a small business had 18 months in which to choose and introduce new finance as well as stock recording and control systems.

- An R&D manager had 8 years to carry through a research program aimed at developing and testing a range of new products to compete with equivalent products known to be coming into the international market. He gave his chief metallurgist 3 years to come up with a range of materials to test and select from. The R&D investigators were in turn assigned specific projects dated for completion in periods ranging from 12 to 18 months.

- A production director had 42 months to move forward the construction of a new building, the installation of plant and equipment, and the recruitment and training of personnel, including dealing with civil authorities, consultants, and contractors.

- A department manager was given 15 months in which to change over to a new production technology and to have it operating profitably.

- A section foreman was given 6 months for the induction and training of three new supervisors who had been promoted from manual jobs.

- A sales director had 4 years in which to develop an international network of sales offices, agents, and warehouses in a company that, until that time, had no experience in extensive export selling.

- A regional sales manager was given 18 months in which to reorganize his region to accommodate two new product lines and the phased transfers of 16 new salesmen and ancillary office staff to his region.

- A first-line salesman had 2 months in which to show a new line of pharmaceutical products to the doctors in his territory.

- A newspaper feature writer had an expense account from his editor allowing him up to a year to make the preparatory contracts and inquiries that would enable him to write a feature article in one week once the issue became hot.[2]

Remember you are seeking only one piece of information: What are the tasks with the longest target completion time in the job? Before examining the significance of this piece of information, let me draw attention to certain critical points that distinguish the time-span measurement from other job-evaluation procedures:

- The longest target completion times in a job are objective pieces of reality; they are not intuitive ratings negotiated by a committee.

- If a manager changes the way he assigns tasks, then the time-span measure will change.

- The time spans in different roles can be compared directly with one another; a 6-month time span is a 6-month time span, regardless of place, job, company, or organization.

Using Time Spans to Manage

Now that we have seen that each job has a time span that can be objectively determined, what does that mean for the management of an organization? With that question in mind, let us examine the three findings mentioned earlier—the correlation of time span with felt-fair pay; the consistency of the emergence of time spans at managerial levels; and, finally, what the time span of discretion means for how individuals feel about their jobs.

TIME SPAN AND FELT-FAIR PAY

For each time-span level there is a corresponding level of pay that people at that level feel to be fair. Regardless of where they work, what they do, or what they earn, all individuals working at the same maximum time span name the same felt-fair pay. The correspondence is extremely high: the correlations in various studies range between 0.85 and 0.92.[3]

This finding holds at all levels from as low as $4.00 per hour to as high as $500,000 per year. It holds for every occupation—managerial, professional, manual, clerical and administrative, research and development, sales, personnel, and so on. It holds throughout a country, or, as in the case of large countries such as the United

States, throughout large sectors such as the Southeast, or the West Coast, or the South, or the Midwest.

Moreover, this finding holds regardless of a person's actual pay. If his actual pay is less than that corresponding to the level generally felt fair for that time span, he feels underpaid. If it is more, he feels overpaid. The relationship is strong.

There have been many tests of this relationship in more than 20 different countries. The most complete testing was carried out in the United States in the mid-1960s at the Minneapolis plant of the Honeywell Corporation, in a 4-year study supervised by Tom Mahoney and Marvin Dunnette from the University of Minnesota.

Roy Richardson, who was then head of management development at Honeywell, carried out the study in a highly controlled research program. He included all the variables that might conceivably affect a person's sense of fair pay for his work in the study. The exhibit "Correlations of Felt-Fair Pay with Job Characteristics" lists the results and shows that time-span measures correlate closely with felt-fair pay and actual pay and reasonably closely with sense of market value. But with the common job evaluation factors such as "know-how," "job impact," "freedom to act," and so on, the correlations are much lower, ranging between 0.45 and 0.25.

Similar systematic studies have been conducted in the United Kingdom, Holland, and Canada, with equally striking correlations ranging between 0.85 and 0.90.[4] Moreover, because the time-span measurement method is objective and unchanging, it can be used at different times. It was possible, for example, to compare the findings of felt-fair pay in an engineering company in the United Kingdom in 1958, with 12 different companies in the United Kingdom in 1968, and with 14 different occupational groups in the National Health Service (nurses, physiotherapists, and so forth) in 1974. When these results are all put together (see the exhibit "Felt-Fair Pay Data Correlated to a Common Baseline at the 1958 Earnings Index") and brought to the same baseline for the changes that occurred in the earnings between 1958 and 1974 (some 303% increase), they fit the same curve closely.

It was these and similar findings that first led to the conclusion that time-span measurement is related to level of work and responsibility as expressed through felt-fair pay. There is another equally strong finding,

Correlations of Felt-Fair Pay with Job Characteristics

Time span	0.86
Actual pay	0.85*
Midpoint of salary range for job grade	0.80
Felt-fair pay (manager)	0.79
Own estimate of market value	0.57
Rating of know-how	0.45
Rating of problem-solving ability	0.42
Rating of time-span planning	0.42
Rating of job impact	0.34
Rating of right responsibility	0.34
Rating of freedom to act	0.25
Age	0.16
Months of service	0.05

*In 19% the actual pay was higher than felt-fair pay

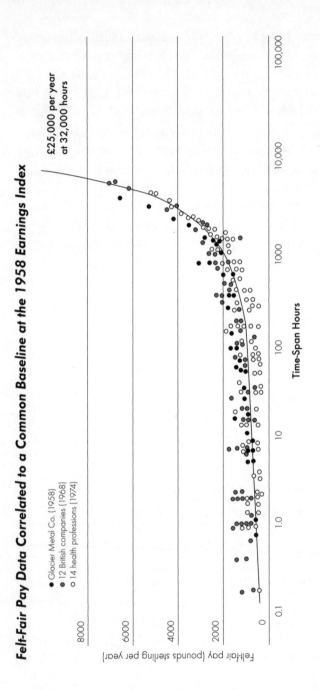

Felt-Fair Pay Data Correlated to a Common Baseline at the 1958 Earnings Index

● Glacier Metal Co. (1958)
● 12 British companies (1968)
○ 14 health professions (1974)

£25,000 per year
at 32,000 hours

Time-Span Hours

Felt-fair pay (pounds sterling per year)

8000

6000

4000

2000

0

0.1   1.0   10   100   1000   10,000   100,000

however, which as far as I am concerned cements the connection. I will now turn to it.

TIME-SPAN LEVELS OF MANAGERIAL WORK

The correlation of time-span levels with felt-fair pay gave the first indication that time-span measurement by itself might be an objective measure of level of work or responsibility. A subsequent discovery at about the same time by Hazekamp and his colleagues at the General Employers Corporation in Holland, and in work at the Glacier Metal Company in England, however, turns out to be even more significant from this point of view.

The finding is that true management levels emerge at the same levels as time spans of discretion. A person must be working at a level *above* 3-months time span if anyone at any level whatever up to 3-months time span will accept him as a manager.

There is another cutoff point to be found at 1-year time span, another at 2 years, then at 5 years, then at 10 years, and probably at 20 years. In the exhibit "True Management Levels Correlated to Time Span," C as well as B will both work with A as their manager regardless of the organization chart. Then B and A will be a real manager-subordinate pair, but B and C will not. C will feel B is "too close" to be his manager, to be "breathing down his neck." Also, regardless of the organization chart, E and F will both really be immediate subordinates of D; P and Q of O; S and T of R.

Another way to look at it is that the more time span of discretion a subordinate has, the more his boss has to have in order to be experienced as a manager. For instance, in this same exhibit, S and T are obvious subordinates of R because they are below the 3-month time

True Management Levels Correlated to Time Span

span and R is above it. E and F are both immediate subordinates of D for the same reason. But for B and C, a 3-month difference is not enough. Because C has a time span of 1 year, B's must be at least 1 year more than C's.

Effective managerial levels end at discrete cutoff points, giving a series of layers of organization in any line of command. As long as only one job sits on any line in each of these layers, a sound managerial system will exist. The trouble starts when two or more positions get pressed into the same line in one layer. People feel crowded in too many managerial levels and on too long lines of command.

These findings are very strong. Reliable data come from over 23 different countries, from industry, commerce, civil services, school systems, social services, hospitals, and administrative services in churches and universities. Everywhere the picture is the same. When organizations are in line with the layers described, the structure will be neither too flat nor too steep.[5] An example of an organization using this underlying organization structure is shown in the exhibit "True Managerial Levels Underlying Organizations."

The existence of these underlying managerial cutoff points in all hierarchies can mean only one thing as far as time-span measures are concerned—that is, the time span itself must be a true measure, by itself, of level of responsibility. Also, the time span of discretion gives us a basic measure for effective organizational design.

(Why the strata of organization should emerge—at the 3-month, 1-year, 2-year, and so forth, time-span levels—is an interesting and important question, the answer to which I venture is related to the nature of human capability in work.)

APPLYING TIME SPAN TO PAY AND GRADING

I have given some indication of how time-span measurement can be used in organization design. It is easy to determine, for example, whether there are too many levels in any part of the organization. Take a number of time-span readings in a given line of command, and, if there is, say, a manager working at a time span of 18 months with an apparent subordinate working at 15 months, then there are too many roles in stratum 3.

Analysis of this kind can help get the whole organization into good trim. There should be only one position in any line of command in each of the organizational strata shown in the exhibit "True Managerial Levels Underlying Organizations."

These work strata or organization levels, however, need to be separated from another system of levels, namely, a system of grades which marks a person's career progression and fixes payment brackets.

True Managerial Levels Underlying Organizations

	Managerial Level	Maximum Number of Subordinates	Time-Span Bracket
Stratum 7	Corporation CEO	150,000	Above 20 years
Stratum 6	Group/division CEO	75,000	10 years to 20 years
Stratum 5	Subsidiary CEO	15,000	5 years to 10 years
Stratum 4	General managers	2,500	2 years to 5 years
Stratum 3	Second line managers	350	1 year to 2 years
Stratum 2	First line managers	50	3 months to one year
Stratum 1	Shop and office floor	–	Up to 3 months

My experience has been that about three times as many grades are required as work strata. The trouble is that ordinarily the two different systems of levels are not distinguished from each other. Usually, a grading system is also used for organizing work, and a command system is violated for grading purposes. As a result, too many organization levels emerge.

The problems can be avoided if the organization is set up in accord with the time span of discretion. The exhibit "Time-Span Strata and Grades," where each work stratum is divided into three grading levels, illustrates this system. Each of the grading levels is marked by a

Time-Span Strata and Grades

Strata				Grades
5 years				
4 years			A	IVA
3 years		B		IVB
2 years	C			IVC
20 months			A	IIIA
16 months		B		IIIB
1 year	C			IIIC
9 months			A	IIA
6 months		B		IIB
3 months	C			IIC
1 month			A	IA
1 week		B		IB
1 day	C			IC
D				ID

specific time-span bracket; for example, stratum 2, which runs from 3-months to 1-year time span, is divided into grades at the 6-month and 9-month time-span levels.

Dividing organizations up in this way may seem like nothing more than a neat and tidy academic exercise. In fact, it is a construction that has practical importance. Let me illustrate.

This system of work strata and grades gives one single uniform system of organization and grading that can be applied throughout the whole enterprise—whether a small company on one site, a large company on many sites, or a multinational in many countries.

If a particular job, regardless of its task, measures in at, say, a 15-month time span, then it is graded IIIC. If another job measures at 21 months, then it is graded IIIA. In this way, all grade IIIC or grade IIIA jobs any-where in the organization are of equivalent size or level of work. They are jobs of the same level regardless of where they are geographically, and whether they are in research, manufacturing, sales, personnel, finance, pro-duction control, electronic data processing, or whatever, and regardless also of their titles.

The universality of time span, therefore, makes it pos-sible to set all job levels within the same framework. This procedure provides a simple and systematic way of nego-tiating and determining pay structures. It is a matter of attaching pay levels to the boundaries of grades.

The equitable pay levels (felt-fair pay levels) for the eastern United States in 1978 are shown in the exhibit "Correlation of Felt-Fair Pay with Time Span." Check the fit of this structure to a current pay and grading system. Take half a dozen jobs, calculate their time spans, and then read off their equitable pay from the exhibit and compare it with their real pay.

Not all the jobs that have the same grade and pay bracket have the same levels in time span. The comparisons, however, will give some idea of the degree of adjustment a pay structure would need if the organization were to move toward time-span grading.

Most subjective methods of evaluating jobs are buttressed by numerous special arrangements for special cases such as scarcity. Experience with the time-span method shows, however, that if full implementation is achieved, fewer of these special arrangements are needed. And if there is genuine evidence of need to pay above the going rate to cope with scarcity, then it is important to do so by adding an explicit scarcity increment, kept separate from the salary—an increment that can be eroded if and when the scarcity disappears.

But, some might ask, what about star performers, perquisites for high-level executives, stock option plans, just simple merit pay raises or differences in performance appraisals, such as when one person in a grade is judged excellent and another merely satisfactory?

The answer here is that good performance is rewarded by merit increases which progress a person through the

Correlation of Felt-Fair Pay with Time Span

Time Span	Felt-Fair Pay, United States 1978 (in thousands of dollars)
10 years	$250,000
5	125,000
2	65,000
1	34,000
3 months	20,000

payment bracket for his grade. If he continues to do very well, and if the required work allows for it, he may be upgraded and then have the chance to move up in pay through the next higher grade. The next move is to recognize substantial growth in a person's ability and performance by promoting him to the next work stratum as opportunities arise. My experience has shown that a systematic pay structure, recognition of work level, effective performance appraisal, and sound progression are the best means for recognizing and rewarding merit. The need to introduce special bonus schemes at any level is usually a reflection of an inadequate salary structure.

The system does not, of course, deal with stars such as actors or professional athletes, or with some special salesmen who are really independent agents, since they are really independent entrepreneurs and not salaried employees.

Time and the Manager

In this article it is not my objective to detail the construction of either organization or payment systems. If I have made the following points well, I will be satisfied:

- Whether one job is bigger than another, has a higher level of responsibility or greater weight of responsibility, can be determined directly by comparing the maximum time span of discretion in the two jobs—the longest times forward in which an incumbent must plan and carry out particular tasks.

- The relationship between time span and level of work shows in two main ways. First, time span coincides uniquely with a person's felt-fair pay regardless of actual pay. Second, time-span measurement reveals a universal underlying structure of management levels, with break points at 3 months, 1 year, 2 years, 5 years, 10 years, 20 years, and higher.

- If management structure is set up with only one role in each work stratum, there is a good chance of getting work programmed and carried through on schedule. Time-span measurement provides for the foundation of a sound and spare managerial structure.

Finally, I pose the question that surely has occurred to the reader of this article. Why does this systematic managerial and payment structure exist in the fiber of employment hierarchies? In answer, I put forward the hypothesis that it has to do with the fact that individual capability expresses itself in time spans and that the distribution of different levels of capability in the working population is at the core of management structures.

Notes

1. For a fuller description, see my book, *Time Span Handbook* (Exeter, NH: Heinemann, 1964).

2. Ibid.

3. Roy Richardson, *Fair Pay and Work* (Exeter, NH: Heinemann, 1971).

4. See, for example, G.E. Krimpas, *Labour Input and the Theory of the Labour Market* (London: Duckworth, 1975).

5. See my book, *A General Theory of Bureaucracy* (New York: Halsted Press, 1976, pp. 133–135).

Originally published in September–October 1979
Reprint 79506

Job Sculpting

The Art of Retaining Your Best People

TIMOTHY BUTLER AND JAMES WALDROOP

Executive Summary

HIRING GOOD PEOPLE IS TOUGH, but keeping them can be even tougher. The professionals streaming out of today's MBA programs are so well educated and achievement oriented that they could do well in virtually any job. But will they stay? According to noted career experts Timothy Butler and James Waldroop, only if their jobs fit their *deeply embedded life interests*—that is, their long-held, emotionally driven passions. Butler and Waldroop identify the eight different life interests of people drawn to business careers and introduce the concept of *job sculpting*, the art of matching people to jobs that resonate with the activities that make them truly happy.

Managers don't need special training to job sculpt, but they do need to listen more carefully when employees describe what they like and dislike about their jobs.

Once managers and employees have discussed deeply embedded life interests—ideally during employee performance reviews—they can work together to customize future work assignments. In some cases, they may mean simply adding another assignment to existing responsibilities. In other cases, it may require moving that employee to a new position altogether.

Skills can be stretched in many directions, but if they are not going in the right direction—one that is congruent with deeply embedded life interests—employees are at risk of becoming dissatisfied and uncommitted. And in an economy where a company's most important asset is the knowledge, energy, and loyalty of its people, that's a large risk to take.

By all accounts, Mark was a star at the large West Coast bank where he had worked for three years. He had an MBA from a leading business school, and he had distinguished himself as an impressive "quant jock" and a skilled lending officer. The bank paid Mark well, and senior managers had every intention of promoting him. Little did they know he was seriously considering leaving the organization altogether.

HIRING GOOD PEOPLE IS TOUGH, but as every senior executive knows, keeping them can be even tougher. Indeed, most executives can tell a story or two about a talented professional who joined their company to great fanfare, added enormous value for a couple of years, and then departed unexpectedly. Usually such exits are written off. "She got an offer she couldn't refuse," you hear, or, "No one stays with one company for very long these days."

Our research over the past 12 years strongly suggests that quite another dynamic is frequently at work. Many talented professionals leave their organizations because senior managers don't understand the psychology of work satisfaction; they assume that people who excel at their work are necessarily happy in their jobs. Sounds logical enough. But the fact is, strong skills don't always reflect or lead to job satisfaction. Many professionals, particularly the leagues of 20- and 30-somethings streaming out of today's MBA programs, are so well educated and achievement oriented that they could succeed in virtually any job. But will they stay?

The answer is, only if the job matches their *deeply embedded life interests*. These interests are not hobbies— opera, skiing, and so forth—nor are they topical enthusiasms, such as Chinese history, the stock market, or oceanography. Instead, deeply embedded life interests are long-held, emotionally driven passions, intricately entwined with personality and thus born of an indeterminate mix of nature and nurture. Deeply embedded life interests do not determine what people are good at— they drive what *kinds* of activities make them happy. At work, that happiness often translates into commitment. It keeps people engaged, and it keeps them from quitting.

In our research, we found only eight deeply embedded life interests for people drawn to business careers. (For a description of each one, see "The Big Eight" at the end of this article.) Life interests start showing themselves in childhood and remain relatively stable throughout our lives, even though they may manifest themselves in different ways at different times. For instance, a child with a nascent deeply embedded life interest in *creative production*—a love for inventing or starting things, or both—may be drawn to writing stories and plays. As a teenager, the life interest might express itself in a hobby of devising mechanical gadgets or an extracurricular pursuit of starting a high school sports or literary magazine. As an adult, the creative-production life interest might bubble up as a drive to be an entre-preneur or a design engineer. It might even show itself as a love for stories again—pushing the person toward a career in, say, producing movies.

Think of a deeply embedded life interest as a geothermal pool of superheated water. It will rise to the surface in one place as a hot spring and in another as a geyser. But beneath the surface—at the core of the individual—the pool is constantly bubbling. Deeply embedded life interests always seem to find expression, even if a person has to change jobs—or careers—for that to happen.

Job sculpting is the art of matching people to jobs that allow their deeply embedded life interests to be expressed. It is the art of forging a customized career path in order to increase the chance of retaining talented people. Make no mistake—job sculpting is challenging; it requires managers to play both detective and psychologist. The reason: many people have only a dim awareness of their own deeply embedded life interests. They may have spent their lives fulfilling other people's expectations of them, or they may have followed the most common career advice: "Do what you're good at." For example, we know of a woman who, on the basis of her skill at chemistry in college, was urged to become a doctor. She complied and achieved great success as a neurologist, but at age 42 she finally quit to open a nursery school. She loved children, demonstrating a deeply embedded life interest in *counseling and mentoring*. And more important, as it turned out, she was also driven by a life interest in *enterprise control*, the desire to be in charge of an organization's overall operations. It was a long time before she stopped remarking, "All those years wasted."

Other people don't know their own deeply embedded life interests because they have taken the path of least resistance: "Well, my dad was a lawyer." Or they've simply been unaware of many career choices at critical points in their lives. Most college seniors and new MBAs set sail on their careers knowing very little about all the possible islands in the sea. And finally, some people end up in the wrong jobs because they have chosen, for reasons good and bad, to follow the siren songs of financial reward or prestige. Regardless of the reason, the fact is that a good number of people, at least up until midlife, don't actually know what kind of work will make them happy. (For more on the importance of life interests, abilities, and values in job satisfaction, see "It's a Matter of Degree" at the end of this article.)

Let's return to Mark, the lending officer at a West Coast bank. Mark was raised in San Francisco; his mother and father were doctors who fully expected their son to become a successful professional. In high school, Mark received straight A's. He went on to attend Princeton, where he majored in economics. Soon after graduation, he began working at a prestigious management consulting firm, where he showed great skill at his assignments: building financial spreadsheets and interpreting pro formas. As expected, Mark left the consulting firm to attend a respected business school and then afterward joined the bank. It was located near his family, and because of its size and growth rate, he thought it would offer him good opportunities for advancement.

Mark, not surprisingly, excelled at every task the bank gave him. He was smart and knew no other way to approach work than to give it his all. But over time, Mark grew more and more unhappy. He was a person who loved running his mind over and through theoretical and strategic what-ifs. (After college, Mark had seriously considered a career in academia but had been dissuaded by his parents.) Indeed, one of Mark's deeply embedded life interests was *theory development and conceptual thinking*. He could certainly excel at the nitty-gritty number crunching and the customer service that his lending job entailed, but those activities did nothing for his heart and soul, not to mention for his commitment to the organization.

Fortunately for both Mark and the bank, he was able to identify what kind of work truly excited him before he quit. Consulting a career counselor, Mark came to see what kind of work interested him and how that differed from his current job responsibilities. Using this insight, he was able to identify a role in the bank's new market development area that would bring his daily tasks in line with his deeply embedded interests. Mark's work now consists of competitive analysis and strategy formulation. He is thriving, and the bank is reaping the benefit of his redoubled energy—and his loyalty.

Career Development: Standard Operating Procedure

As we've said, managers botch career development—and retention—because they mistakenly assume people are satisfied with jobs they excel at. But there are other reasons why career development goes wrong. The first is the way jobs usually get filled, and the second is the fact that career development so often gets handed off to the human resources department.

Most people get moved or promoted in their organizations according to a preset schedule—a new assignment every 18 months, say—or when another position in the company opens up. In either case, managers must scramble. If six employees are all scheduled to get new assignments on August 1, for example, a manager has to play mix and match, and usually does so based on abilities. Who is likely, the manager will ask herself, to do best in which jobs? Similarly, when a position opens up and needs to be filled right away, a manager must ask, "What skills does the job require? Who has them or seems most likely to develop them quickly?"

Sometimes people move up in an organization because they demand it. A talented employee might, for example, inform his manager that he wants to graduate to a new role because he's not growing anymore. The typical manager then considers the employee's skills and tries to find a place in the organization where they can be applied again, this time with a bit of "stretch."

Stretch assignments, however, often do little to address deeply embedded life interests. A research assistant at an investment management firm who performs well can stretch her skills into a credit analyst role, and after continued success there, she can move into the position of fixed-income portfolio manager. But what if her deeper interests are in managing others? Or how about the "spot news" reporter who is "stretched" into management when her real passion (discovered, perhaps, through a few years of misadventure as a manager) lies in investigative reporting?

Skills can be stretched in many directions, but if they are not going in a direction that is congruent with deeply embedded life interests, then employees are at risk of becoming dissatisfied and uncommitted. In such situations, employees usually attribute their unhappiness to their managers or to their organizations. They'll decide their organization has the wrong culture, for example. That kind of thinking often leads to a "migration cure" of leaving one organization for another, only to find similar dissatisfaction because the root of the career malaise has not been identified and addressed. One individual we consulted, a manager in the high-tech industry, went through three companies before realizing it wasn't the company he needed to change but his work. He had never wanted to be a manager but had agreed to a promotion because it offered more money and prestige. All he really wanted to do was design intricate machinery and mechanisms; he wanted to be an engineer again.

That story brings us to the second reason career development is handled poorly. The engineer was originally promoted to manager at the suggestion of the human resources department. Generally speaking, we have found that when career development is handed off to HR, problems arise. Many HR managers try to tackle career development using standardized tests such as the Myers-Briggs Type Indicator. There is nothing wrong with the Myers-Briggs and tests like it. In fact, they are excellent when used to help teams understand their own working dynamics. But personality type should not be the foundation of career development. Some HR managers do use the Strong Interest Inventory to get at life interests, which is better, but it suffers from being too general. The Strong helps people who want to know if they should be a Marine Corps sergeant or a ballet dancer, but it does little for people who say, "I know I want to work in business. Exactly what type of job is best for me?"

The bigger problem with allowing HR to handle career development is that it cuts the manager out of the process. Career development in general, and job sculpting in particular, requires an ongoing dialogue between an employee and his boss; it should not be shunted to another department, however good it may be. HR adds its value in training and supporting managers as career developers.

The Techniques of Job Sculpting

Job sculpting, then, begins when managers identify each employee's deeply embedded life interests. Sometimes an employee's life interest is glaringly obvious—she is excited doing one kind of work and dismal doing another. But much more often, a manager has to probe and observe.

Some managers worry that job sculpting requires them to play psychologist. They shouldn't worry. If they're good managers, they already play the role of psychologist intuitively. Managers *should* have a strong interest in the motivational psychology of their employees. In fact, they should openly express their willingness to help sculpt their employees' careers and to make the extra effort required to hold onto talented people.

Job sculpting, incidentally, can also be marketed externally to attract new hires. We have an unusual vantage point: we've seen close to a thousand new business professionals recruited and hired every year for the last 20 years. Without a doubt, the single most important thing on the minds of new MBAs is—not money!—but whether a position will move their long-term careers in a chosen direction. In fact, during a recent recruiting season, one employer—a Wall Street firm—gained a significant advantage over its competitors by emphasizing its commitment to career development. In both presentations and individual discussions, executives from the firm described its interest in and commitment to helping its professionals think about and manage their careers— a fact that many students cited as key to their choosing that firm.

If managers promise to job sculpt, of course they have to deliver. But how? Each change in assignment provides an opportunity to do some sculpting. For instance, a salesperson with an interest in *quantitative analysis* might be given new duties working with the marketing product manager and market research analysts—while remaining in sales. Or an engineer with an interest in *influence through language and ideas* might be given the task of helping the marketing communications people design sales support materials or user manuals—again, while retaining her primary role as an engineer.

But we have found that such intermittent patching attempts at job sculpting are not nearly as effective as bringing the process directly into the regular performance review. An effective performance review dedicates time to discussing past performance and plans for the future. In making job sculpting part of those conversations, it becomes systematized, and in becoming systematized, the chances of someone's career "falling through the cracks" are minimized.

Do managers need special training to job sculpt? No, but they do need to start listening more carefully when employees describe what they like and dislike about their jobs. Consider the case of a pharmaceutical company executive who managed 30 salespeople. In a performance review, one of her people offhandedly mentioned that her favorite part of the past year had been helping their division find new office space and negotiating for its lease. "That was a blast. I loved it," she told her boss. In the past, the executive would have paid the comment little heed. After all, what did it have to do with the woman's performance in sales? But listening with the ears of a job sculptor, the executive probed further, asking, "What made the search for new office space fun for you?" and "How was that different from what you do day-to-day?" The conversation revealed that the saleswoman was actually very dissatisfied and bored with her current position and was considering leaving. In fact, the saleswoman yearned for work that met her deeply embedded life interests, which had to do with *influence through language and ideas* and *creative production.* Her sales job encompassed the former, but it was only when she had the chance to think about the location, design, and layout of the new office that her creativity could be fully expressed. The manager helped the woman move to a position at company headquarters, where her primary responsibility was to design marketing and advertising materials.

Along with listening carefully and asking probing questions during the performance review, managers can ask employees to play an active role in job sculpting— before the meeting starts. In most corporate settings, the employee's preparation for a performance review includes a written assessment of accomplishments, goals for the upcoming review period, skill areas in need of development, and plans for accomplishing both goals and growth. During the review, this assessment is then compared to the supervisor's assessment.

But imagine what would happen if employees were also expected to write up their personal views of career satisfaction. Imagine if they were to prepare a few paragraphs on what kind of work they love or if they described their favorite activities on the job. Because so many people are unaware of their deeply embedded life interests—not to mention unaccustomed to discussing them with their managers—such exercises might not come easily at first. Yet they would be an excellent starting point for a discussion, ultimately allowing employees to speak more clearly about what they want from work, both in the short and long term. And that information would make even the best job-sculpting managers more effective.

Once managers and employees have discussed deeply embedded life interests, it's time to customize the next work assignment accordingly. In cases where the employee requires only a small change in his activities, that might just mean adding a new responsibility. For example, an engineer who has a deeply embedded life interest in *counseling and mentoring* might be asked to plan and manage the orientation of new hires. Or a logistics planner with a deeply embedded life interest in *influence through language and ideas* could be given the task of working on recruitment at college campuses. The goals here would be to give some immediate gratification through an immediate and real change in the job and to begin the process of moving the individual to a role that more fully satisfies him.

Sometimes, however, job sculpting calls for more substantial changes. Mark, the dissatisfied bank lending officer is one example. Another is Carolyn, who was a star industry analyst at a leading Wall Street firm. Carolyn was so talented at designing and using sophisticated new quantitative approaches to picking stocks that at one point the head of the entire division remarked, "Carolyn has brought our business into the twenty-first century." That same year, she was ranked as the second most valuable person within the entire group—out of almost a hundred very talented finance professionals. For the past several years, senior managers had sought to ensure Carolyn's loyalty to the organization by awarding her generous raises and bonuses, making her one of their highest paid people.

But Carolyn had one foot out the door. When she received a huge raise (even by the standards of this firm and her own compensation history), she was actually angry, commenting to a friend, "That's typical of this company; it thinks that it can solve every problem by throwing money at it." Although she loved analysis and mathematics, she had a strong desire to have a greater impact on the decision making and direction of the research group. She had definite opinions regarding what kind of people they should be hiring, how the group should be organized and the work assigned, and how the group could most effectively work with other departments—in other words, she had deeply embedded life interests in *enterprise control* and *managing people and relationships.*

A performance review gave Carolyn a chance to express her dreams and frustrations to her boss. Together they arrived at a "player-coach" role for Carolyn as coordinator of research. She was still an analyst, but she also had taken on the responsibilities of guiding and directing several teams, making decisions about hiring and promotions, and helping set strategic direction.

A year later, all parties agreed that the research group had never been more productive.

Job sculpting allowed Carolyn's firm to keep some of her extraordinary skills as an analyst while satisfying her desire to manage. But oftentimes job sculpting involves more sacrifice on the part of the organization. Remember that when Mark moved to his new job in business development, the bank lost a talented lending officer. Sometimes job sculpting requires short-term pain for long-term gain, although we would argue that in Mark's case—and in many others like it—they would have lost him soon enough anyway.

And one final caveat emptor. When job sculpting requires taking away parts of a job an employee dislikes, it also means finding someone new to take them on. If staffing levels are sufficient, that won't be a problem—an uninteresting part of one person's job may be perfect for someone else. At other times, however, there won't be a knight in shining armor to take on the "discarded" work. And at still other times, a manager may recognize that there is simply no way to accomplish the job sculpting the employee wants or even needs. (For instance, an engineering firm may not have activities to satisfy a person with a life interest in *influence through language and ideas*.) In such a case, a manager may have to make the hard choice to counsel a talented employee to leave the company.

Even with its challenges, job sculpting is worth the effort. In the knowledge economy, a company's most important asset is the energy and loyalty of its people— the intellectual capital that, unlike machines and factories, can quit and go to work for your competition. And yet, many managers regularly undermine that commitment by allowing talented people to stay in jobs they're doing well at but aren't fundamentally interested in. That just doesn't make sense. To turbocharge retention, you must first know the hearts and minds of your employees and then undertake the tough and rewarding task of sculpting careers that bring joy to both.

The Big Eight

WE HAVE FOUND THAT MOST people in business are motivated by between one and three deeply embedded life interests—long-held, emotionally driven passions for certain kinds of activities. Deeply embedded life interests are not hobbies or enthusiasms; they are innate passions that are intricately entwined with personality. Life interests don't determine what we're good at but what kinds of work we love.

Our conclusions about the number and importance of deeply embedded life interests have grown out of more than a decade of research into the drivers of career satisfaction. In 1986, we began interviewing professionals from a wide range of industries and functions as well as asking them to take a battery of psychological tests in order to assess what factors contributed to work satisfaction. Over the next dozen years, our database had grown to 650 people.

The results of our research were striking: scales on several of the tests we used clearly formed eight separate clusters. In other words, all business work could be broken down into eight types of core activities. By looking more closely at the content of the scales in each cluster and by cross-referencing this information to our interview data and counseling experience, we developed and tested a model of what we call "business core functions." These core functions represent the way deeply embedded life interests find expression in business. The following is a summary of each:

Application of Technology

Whether or not they are actually working as—or were trained to be—engineers, people with the life interest application of technology are intrigued by the inner workings of things. They are curious about finding better ways to use technology to solve business problems. We know a successful money manager who acts as his company's unofficial computer consultant because he loves the challenge of unlocking code. Indeed, he loves it more than his "day job"! People with the application-of-technology life interest often enjoy work that involves planning and analyzing production and operations systems and redesigning business processes.

It's often easy to recognize people with a strong application-of-technology life interest. They speak fondly of their college years when they majored in computer science or engineering. They read software magazines and manuals for fun. They comment excitedly when the company installs new hardware.

But sometimes the signs are more subtle. Application-of-technology people often approach business problems with a "let's take this apart and solve it" mind-set. And when introduced to a new process at work, they like to get under the hood and fully understand how it works rather than just turn the key and drive it. In a snapshot, application-of-technology people are the ones who want to know how a clock works because the technology excites them—as does the possibility that it could be tinkered with and perhaps improved.

Quantitative Analysis

Some people aren't just good at running the numbers, they excel at it. They see it as the best, and sometimes the only, way to figure out business solutions. Similarly, they see mathematical work as fun when others consider it drudgery, such as performing a cash-flow analysis, forecasting the future performance of an investment instrument, or figuring out the best debt/equity structure for a business. They might also enjoy building computer models in order to determine optimal production scheduling and to perform accounting procedures.

Not all "quant jocks" are in jobs that reflect this deeply embedded life interest. In fact, many of these individuals find themselves in other kinds of work because they have been told that following their true passion will narrow their career prospects. Yet these people are not difficult to miss, because regardless of their assignment, they gravitate toward numbers. Consider the HR professional who analyzes his organization by looking at compensation levels and benefits and by studying the ratio of managers to employees. Similarly, a marketing manager who loves analyzing customer research data—versus the subjective findings of focus groups—is probably a person with quantitative analysis at her core.

Theory Development and Conceptual Thinking

For some people, nothing brings more enjoyment than thinking and talking about abstract ideas. Think of Mark, the West Coast banker who was frustrated in his position because he did not have the opportunity to ponder big-picture strategy. Like Mark, people with this deeply embedded life interest are drawn to theory—the why of strategy interests them much more than the how. People with this interest can be excited by building business models that explain competition within a given industry or by analyzing the competitive position of a business within a particular market. Our research also shows that people with this deeply embedded interest are often drawn to academic careers. Some end up there; many do not.

How can you identify the people with this interest? For starters, they're not only conversant in the language of theory, but they also genuinely enjoy talking about abstract concepts. Often, these are the people who like thinking about situations from the "30,000 foot" level. Another clue: these individuals often subscribe to periodicals that have an academic bent.

Creative Production

Some people always enjoy the beginning of projects the most, when there are many unknowns and they can make something out of nothing. These individuals are frequently seen as imaginative, out-of-the-box thinkers. They seem most engaged when they are brainstorming or inventing unconventional solutions. Indeed, they seem to thrive on newness. The reason: creative production is one of their dominant deeply embedded life interests— making something original, be it a product or a process.

Our research shows that many entrepreneurs, R&D scientists, and engineers have this life interest. Many of them have an interest in the arts, but just as many don't. An entrepreneur we know has virtually no passion for the arts; his quite successful businesses over the years have included manufacturing decidedly unsexy paper bags and sealing tape.

There are, of course, many places in the business world where people with this interest can find satisfying work—new product development, for example, or advertising. Many people with this interest gravitate toward creative industries such as entertainment. Yet others, like one investment analyst we know, repress this life interest because they feel that it is "too soft" for business. Creative production, they believe, is for their off-hours.

Fortunately for managers, most creative-production people are not terribly hard to recognize. They wear their life interest on their sleeves—sometimes literally, by virtue of their choice of unconventional clothing, but almost always by how excited they are when talking about the new elements of a business or product. Oftentimes, they show little interest in things that are already established, no matter how profitable or state-of-the-art.

Counseling and Mentoring

For some people, nothing is more enjoyable than teaching—in business, that usually translates into coaching or mentoring. These individuals are driven by the deeply embedded life interest of counseling and mentoring, allowing them to guide employees, peers, and even clients to better performance. People with a high interest in counseling and mentoring are also often drawn to organizations, such as museums, schools, and hospitals, that provide products or services they perceive to hold a high social value. People like to counsel and mentor for many reasons. Some derive satisfaction when other people succeed; others love the feeling of being needed. Regardless, these people are drawn to work where they can help others grow and improve. We know, for instance, of a brand manager at a consumer goods company who was primarily responsible for designing her product's marketing and distribution plans. Yet she eagerly made time every week to meet one-on-one with several subordinates in order to provide feedback on their performance and answer any questions they had about the company and their careers. When it came time for her performance review, the brand manager's boss didn't bother to evaluate this counseling-and-mentoring work, saying that it wasn't technically part of the brand manager's job. It was, however, her favorite part.

People with a counseling-and-mentoring interest will make themselves known if their jobs include the opportunity to do so. But many people in this category don't get that chance. (New MBAs, in particular, are not asked to coach other employees for several years out.) However, you can sometimes identify counseling-and-mentoring people by their hobbies and volunteer work. Many are drawn to hands-on community service, such as the Big Brother Organization or literacy programs. People with a high interest in counseling and mentoring can be recognized by the fact that when they talk about their previous work they often talk fondly about the people who worked under them and where they are now—like a parent would talk about his or her children.

Managing People and Relationships

Longing to counsel and mentor people is one thing; wanting to manage them is another thing entirely. Individuals with this deeply embedded life interest enjoy dealing with people on a day-to-day basis. They derive a lot of satisfaction from workplace relationships—but they focus much more on outcomes than do people in the counseling-and-mentoring category. In other words, they're less interested in seeing people grow than in working with and through them to accomplish the goals of the business, whether it be building a product or making a sale. That is why people with this life interest often find happiness in line management positions or in sales careers.

Take Tom, a 32-year-old Harvard MBA who joined an Internet start-up in Silicon Valley—mainly because that was what all his classmates were doing. Tom had an undergraduate degree and work experience in engineering, and so his new company put him right to work in its technology division. Tom had no subordinates and no clients and mainly spent his days talking to other engineers and testing prototypes. It was the perfect job for someone with Tom's background, but not for someone with his life interest in managing people and relationships. After six months, he was miserable.

Tom was about to quit when the company announced it needed someone to help set up and run a new manufacturing plant in Texas. Tom pounced on the job—he would ultimately be leading a staff of 300 and negotiating frequently with suppliers. He got the job and still holds it today, five years later. His desire to motivate, organize, and direct people has been happily fulfilled.

Enterprise Control

Sarah, an attorney, is a person who has loved running things ever since she was a child. At age five, she set up her first lemonade stand and refused to let her older brother and sister help pour the juice, set prices, or collect money. (She did, however, let them flag down customers.) As a teenager, Sarah ran a summer camp in her backyard. And in college, she was the president of not one but three major groups, including the student government.

People accuse her of being a control freak, and Sarah doesn't argue—she is happiest when she has ultimate decision-making authority. She feels great when she is in charge of making things happen.

Wanting too much control can be unhealthy, both for the people themselves and for their organizations, but some people are driven—in quite healthy ways—by a deeply embedded life interest in enterprise control. Whether or not they like managing people, these people find satisfaction in making the decisions that determine the direction taken by a work team, a business unit, a company division, or an entire organization. Sarah was not particularly happy as a lawyer—a career she pursued at the behest of an influential college instructor, and her mother, a lawyer herself. But she did eventually fulfill her life interest in enterprise control when, after coming back from maternity leave, she asked to run the company's New York office, with 600 attorneys, clerks, and other staff. It was, she says, "a match made in heaven."

Enterprise-control people are easy to spot in organizations. They seem happiest when running projects or teams; they enjoy "owning" a transaction such as a trade or a sale. These individuals also tend to ask for as much responsibility as possible in any work situation. Pure interest in enterprise control can be seen as an interest in deal making or in strategy—a person with this life interest wants to be the CEO, not the COO. Investment bankers, for example, don't run ongoing operations but often demonstrate a very strong interest in enterprise control.

Influence Through Language and Ideas

Some people love ideas for their own sake, but others love expressing them for the sheer enjoyment that comes from storytelling, negotiating, or persuading. Such are people with the deeply embedded life interest of influence through language and ideas. They feel most fulfilled when they are writing or speaking—or both. Just let them communicate.

People in this category sometimes feel drawn to careers in public relations or advertising, but they often find themselves elsewhere, because speaking and writing are largely considered skills, not careers. And yet for some, effective communication is more than just a skill—it's a passion. One way to identify these individuals in your organization is to notice who volunteers for writing assignments. One MBA student we counseled joined a large consulting firm where, for three years, she did the standard analytical work of studying industry dynamics and so forth. When she heard that a partner had to create a report for a new client "that liked to see things in writing," she quickly offered her services. Her report was so persuasive—and she had such a fun experience writing it—that she was soon writing for the company full-time. Had her deeply embedded interest in communication not been met in-house, she surely would have sought it elsewhere.

People with strong interests in influence through language and ideas love persuasion of all sorts, spoken and written, verbal and visual. They enjoy thinking about their audience (whether one person or millions) and the best way to address them. And they enjoy spending time on communications both outside and inside the company. One woman we know who is the head of strategic planning for an entertainment company says, "I spend at least 75% of my time thinking about how to sell our findings to the CEO and other members of the executive team." Clearly, the amount of mental energy this executive devotes to persuasion characterizes her as an influence-through-language-and-ideas person.

As we've noted, it is not uncommon for managers to sense that an employee has more than one deeply embedded life interest. That is possible. The pairs of life interests that are most commonly found together are listed below:

- *Enterprise Control* **with** *Managing People and Relationships.* These individuals want to run a business on a day-to-day basis but are also challenged by—and enjoy—managing people.

- *Managing People and Relationships* **with** *Counseling and Mentoring.* These are the ultimate people-oriented professionals. They have a strong preference for service-management roles, enjoying the frontline aspects of working in high customer-contact environments. They also tend to enjoy human resources management roles.

- *Quantitative Analysis* **with** *Managing People and Relationships.* These individuals like finance and finance-related jobs, yet they also find a lot of pleasure managing people toward goals.

- *Enterprise Control* **with** *Influence Through Language and Ideas.* This is the most common profile of people who enjoy sales. (An interest in Managing People and Relationships is also often high among satisfied salespeople.) This combination is also found extensively among general managers—especially those who are charismatic leaders.

- *Application of Technology* **with** *Managing People and Relationships.* This is the engineer, computer scientist, or other technically oriented individual who enjoys leading a team.

- **Creative Production** with **Enterprise Control.** This is the most common combination among entrepreneurs. These people want to start things and dictate where projects will go. "Give me the ball and I'll score" is their mantra.

It's a Matter of Degree

OVER THE PAST SEVERAL DECADES, countless studies have been conducted to discover what makes people happy at work. The research almost always focuses on three variables: ability, values, and life interests. In this article, we argue that life interests are paramount—but what of the other two? Don't they matter? The answer is yes, but less so.

Ability—meaning the skills, experience, and knowledge a person brings to the job—can make an employee feel competent. That's important; after all, research has shown that a feeling of incompetence hinders creativity, not to mention productivity. But although competence can certainly help a person get hired, its effect is generally short lived. People who are good at their jobs aren't necessarily engaged by them.

In the context of career satisfaction, values refer to the rewards people seek. Some people value money, others want intellectual challenge, and still others desire prestige or a comfortable lifestyle. People with the same abilities and life interests may pursue different careers based on their values. Take three people who excel at and love quantitative analysis. One might pursue a career as a professor of finance for the intellectual challenge. Another might go straight to Wall Street to reap the financial rewards. And a third might pursue whatever job track leads to the CEO's office—driven by a desire for power and influence.

Like ability, values matter. In fact, people rarely take jobs that don't match their values. A person who hates to travel would not jump at an offer from a management consulting firm. Someone who values financial security won't chase a career as an independent contractor. But people can be drawn into going down career paths because they have the ability and like the rewards—even though they're not interested in the work. After a short period of success, they become disenchanted, lose interest, and either quit or just work less productively.

That's why we have concluded that life interests are the most important of the three variables of career satisfaction. You can be good at a job—indeed, you generally need to be—and you can like the rewards you receive from it. But only life interests will keep most people happy and fulfilled over the long term. And that's the key to retention.

Originally published in September–October 1999
Reprint 99502

The Young and the Clueless

KERRY A. BUNKER, KATHY E. KRAM, AND
SHARON TING

Executive Summary

IT'S NATURAL TO PROMOTE your best and brightest,
especially when you think they may leave for greener
pastures if you don't continually offer them new challenges and rewards. But promoting smart, ambitious
young managers too quickly often robs them of the
chance to develop the emotional competencies that
come with time and experience—competencies like the
ability to negotiate with peers, regulate emotions in times
of crisis, and win support for change. Indeed, at some
point in a manager's career—usually at the vice president
level—raw talent and ambition become less important
than the ability to influence and persuade, and that's the
point at which the emotionally immature manager will
lose his effectiveness.

This article argues that delaying a promotion can
sometimes be the best thing a senior executive can do

for a junior manager. The inexperienced manager who is given time to develop his emotional competencies may be better prepared for the interpersonal demands of top-level leadership. The authors recommend that senior executives employ these strategies to help boost their protégés' people skills: sharpen the 360-degree feedback process, give managers cross-functional assignments to improve their negotiation skills, make the development of emotional competencies mandatory, make emotional competencies a performance measure, and encourage managers to develop informal learning partnerships with peers and mentors.

Delaying a promotion can be difficult given the steadfast ambitions of many junior executives and the hectic pace of organizational life. It may mean going against the norm of promoting people almost exclusively on smarts and business results. It may also mean contending with the disappointment of an esteemed subordinate. But taking the time to build people's emotional competencies isn't an extravagance; it's critical to developing effective leaders.

IN MANY WAYS, 36-year-old Charles Armstrong is a natural leader. He's brilliant, creative, energetic, aggressive—a strategic and financial genius. He's risen quickly through the ranks due to his keen business instincts and proven ability to deliver bottom-line results, at times jumping from one organization to another to leapfrog through the hierarchy. But now his current job is on the line. A division president at an international consumer products company, he's just uncovered a major production setback on a heavily promoted new product. Thousands of orders have been delayed, customers are furious, and the company's stock price has plummeted since the news went public.

Worse, the crisis was utterly preventable. Had Armstrong understood the value of building relationships with his peers and had his subordinates found him approachable, he might have been able to appreciate the cross-functional challenges of developing this particular product. He might have learned of the potential delay months earlier instead of at the eleventh hour. He could have postponed a national advertising campaign and set expectations with investors. He might have even found a way to solve the problems and launch the product on time. But despite his ability to dazzle his superiors with talent and intellect, Armstrong is widely viewed by his peers and subordinates as self-promoting, intolerant, and remote. Perhaps worse, he's only half aware of how others perceive him, and to the extent he does know, he's not terribly concerned. These relationships are not a priority for him. Like so many other talented young managers, Armstrong lacks the emotional competencies that would enable him to work more effectively as part of a team. And now his bosses seem to have unwittingly undermined his career, having promoted him too quickly, before he could develop the relationship skills he needs.

Break the Pattern

What happened with Charles Armstrong is an increasingly common phenomenon. In the past ten years, we've met dozens of managers who have fallen victim to a harmful mix of their own ambition and their bosses' willingness to overlook a lack of people skills.

(As with all the examples in these pages, we've changed Armstrong's name and other identifying features to protect our clients' identities.) Indeed, most executives seek out smart, aggressive people, paying more attention to their accomplishments than to their emotional maturity. What's more, they know that their strongest performers have options—if they don't get the job they want at one company, they're bound to get it somewhere else. Why risk losing them to a competitor by delaying a promotion?

The answer is that promoting them can be just as risky. Putting these unseasoned managers into positions of authority too quickly robs them of the opportunity to develop the emotional competencies that come with time and experience—competencies like the ability to negotiate with peers, regulate their emotions in times of crisis, or win support for change. Bosses may be delighted with such managers' intelligence and passion—and may even see younger versions of themselves—but peers and subordinates are more likely to see them as arrogant and inconsiderate, or, at the very least, aloof. And therein lies the problem. At some point in a young manager's career, usually at the vice president level, raw talent and determined ambition become less important than the ability to influence and persuade. And unless senior executives appreciate this fact and make emotional competence a top priority, these high-potential managers will continue to fail, often at significant cost to the company.

Research has shown that the higher a manager rises in the ranks, the more important soft leadership skills are to his success.[1] Our colleagues at the Center for Creative Leadership have found that about a third of senior executives derail or plateau at some point, most often due to an emotional deficit such as the inability to build a team or regulate their own emotions in times of stress. And in our combined 55 years of coaching and teaching, we've seen firsthand how a young manager risks his career when he fails to develop emotional competencies. But the problem isn't youth per se. The problem is a lack of emotional maturity, which doesn't come easily or automatically and isn't something you learn from a book. It's one thing to understand the importance of relationships at an intellectual level and to learn techniques like active listening; it's another matter entirely to develop a full range of interpersonal competencies like patience, openness, and empathy. Emotional maturity involves a fundamental shift in self-awareness and behavior, and that change requires practice, diligence, and time.

Armstrong's boss admits that he may have promoted the young manager too soon: "I was just like Charles when I was his age, but I was a director, not a division president. It's easier to make mistakes and learn when you aren't in such a big chair. I want him to succeed, and I think he could make a great CEO one day, but sometimes he puts me at risk. He's just too sure of himself to listen." And so, in many cases, executives do their employees and the company a service by delaying the promotion of a young manager and giving him the chance to develop his interpersonal skills. Interrupting the manager's ascent long enough to round out his experience will usually yield a much more effective and stable leader.

This article will look at five strategies for boosting emotional competencies and redirecting managers who are paying a price for damaged or nonexistent relationships. The strategies aren't terribly complicated, but implementing them and getting people to change their entrenched behaviors can be very difficult. Many of these managers are accustomed to receiving accolades, and it often isn't easy for them to hear—or act on—difficult messages. You may have to satisfy yourself with small victories and accept occasional slipups. But perhaps the greatest challenge is having the discipline to resist the charm of the young and the clueless—to refrain from promoting them before they are ready and to stay the course even if they threaten to quit. (For more information, see "Think Before Promoting" at the end of this article.)

DEEPEN 360-DEGREE FEEDBACK

With its questionnaires and standardized rating scales, 360-degree feedback as it is traditionally implemented may not be sufficiently specific or detailed to get the attention of inexperienced managers who excel at bottom-line measures but struggle with more subtle relationship challenges. These managers will benefit from a deeper and more thorough process that includes time for reflection and follow-up conversations. That means, for example, interviewing a wider range of the manager's peers and subordinates and giving her the opportunity to read verbatim responses to open-ended questions. Such detailed and extensive feedback can help a person see herself more as others do, a must for the young manager lacking the self-awareness to understand where she's falling short.

We witnessed this lack of self-awareness in Bill Miller, a 42-year-old vice president at a software company—an environment where technical ability is highly prized. Miller had gone far on pure intellect, but he never fully appreciated his own strengths. So year after year, in assignment after assignment, he worked doubly hard at learning the complexities of the business, neglecting his relationships with his colleagues as an unintended consequence. His coworkers considered his smarts and business acumen among the finest in the company, but they found him unapproachable and detached. As a result, top management questioned his ability to lead the type of strategic change that would require motivating staff at all levels. Not until Miller went through an in-depth 360-degree developmental review was he able to accept that he no longer needed to prove his intelligence—that he could relax in that respect and instead work on strengthening his personal connections. After months of working hard to cultivate stronger relationships with his employees, Miller began to notice that he felt more included in chance social encounters like hallway conversations.

Art Grainger, a 35-year-old senior manager at a cement and concrete company, was generally considered a champion by his direct reports. He was also known for becoming defensive whenever his peers or superiors questioned or even discussed his unit's performance. Through 360-degree reviews, he discovered that while everyone saw him as committed, results-oriented, and technically brilliant, they also saw him as overly protective, claiming he resisted any action or decision that might affect his department. Even his employees felt that he kept them isolated from the rest of the company, having said he reviewed all memos between departments, didn't invite people from other parts of the company to his department's meetings, and openly criticized other managers. Only when Grainger heard that his staff agreed with what his bosses had been telling him for years did he concede that he needed to change. Since then, he has come to see members of other departments as potential allies and has tried to redefine his team to include people from across the company.

It's worth noting that many of these smart young managers aren't used to hearing criticism. Consequently, they may discount negative feedback, either because the comments don't mesh with what they've heard in previous conversations or because their egos are so strong. Or they may conclude that they can "fix" the problem right away—after all, they've been able to fix most problems they've encountered in the past. But developing emotional competencies requires practice and ongoing personal interactions. The good news is that if you succeed in convincing them that these issues are career threatening, they may apply the same zeal to their emotional development that they bring to their other projects. And that's why 360-degree feedback is so valuable: When it comes from multiple sources and is ongoing, it's difficult to ignore.

INTERRUPT THE ASCENT

When people are continually promoted within their areas of expertise, they don't have to stray far from their comfort zones, so they seldom need to ask for help, especially if they're good problem solvers. Accordingly, they may become overly independent and fail to cultivate relationships with people who could be useful to them in the future. What's more, they may rely on the authority that comes with rank rather than learning how to influence people. A command-and-control mentality may work in certain situations, particularly in lower to middle management, but it's usually insufficient in more senior positions, when peer relationships are critical and success depends more on the ability to move hearts and minds than on the ability to develop business solutions.

We sometimes counsel our clients to broaden young managers' skills by assigning them to cross-functional roles outside their expected career paths. This is distinct from traditional job rotation, which has employees spending time in different functional areas to enhance and broaden their knowledge of the business. Rather, the manager is assigned a role in which he doesn't have much direct authority. This will help him focus on developing other skills like negotiation and influencing peers.

Consider the case of Sheila McIntyre, a regional sales director at a technology company. McIntyre had been promoted quickly into the managerial ranks because she consistently outsold her colleagues month after month. In her early thirties, she began angling for another promotion—this time, to vice president—but her boss, Ron Meyer, didn't think she was ready. Meyer felt that McIntyre had a quick temper and little patience for people whom she perceived as less visionary. So he put the promotion on hold, despite McIntyre's stellar performance, and created a yearlong special assignment for her— heading a team investigating cross-selling opportunities. To persuade her to take the job, he not only explained that it would help McIntyre broaden her skills but promised a significant financial reward if she succeeded, also hinting that the hoped-for promotion would follow. It was a stretch for McIntyre. She had to use her under-developed powers of persuasion to win support from managers in other divisions. But in the end, her team presented a brilliant cross-selling strategy, which the company implemented over the following year. More important, she developed solid relationships with a number of influential people throughout the organization and learned a lot about the value of others' insights and experiences. McIntyre was eventually promoted to vice president, and to Meyer's satisfaction, her new reports now see her not just as a superstar salesperson but as a well-connected manager who can negotiate on their behalf.

Such cross-functional assignments—with no clear authority or obvious ties to a career path—can be a tough sell. It's not easy to convince young managers that these assignments are valuable, nor is it easy to help them extract relevant knowledge. If the managers feel marginalized, they may not stick around. Remember Bill Miller, the vice president who had neglected his emotional skills in his zeal to learn the business? While he was successful in some of his early informal attempts to build relationships, he was confused and demoralized when his boss, Jerry Schulman, gave him a special assignment to lead a task force reviewing internal processes. Miller had expected a promotion, and the new job didn't feel "real." Schulman made the mistake of not telling Miller that he saw the job as an ideal networking opportunity, so Miller began to question his future at the company. A few months into the new job, Miller gave his notice. He seized an opportunity—a step up—at an arch-rival, taking a tremendous amount of talent and institutional knowledge with him. Had Schulman shared his reasoning with Miller, he might have retained one of his most valuable players—one who had already seen the importance of developing his emotional competence and had begun to make progress.

ACT ON YOUR COMMITMENT

One of the reasons employees get stuck in the pattern we've described is that their bosses point out deficits in emotional competencies but don't follow through. They either neglect to articulate the consequences of continuing the destructive behavior or make empty threats but proceed with a promotion anyway. The hard-charging young executive can only conclude that these competencies are optional.

A cautionary tale comes from Mitchell Geller who, at 29, was on the verge of being named partner at a law firm. He had alienated many of his peers and subordinates over the years through his arrogance, a shortcoming duly noted on his yearly performance reviews, yet his keen legal mind had won him promotion after promotion. With Geller's review approaching, his boss, Larry Snow, pointed to heavy attrition among the up-and-coming lawyers who worked for Geller and warned him that further advancement would be contingent on a change in personal style. Geller didn't take the feedback to heart—he was confident that he'd get by, as he always had, on sheer talent. And true to form, Snow didn't stick to his guns. The promotion came through even though Geller's behavior hadn't changed. Two weeks later, Geller, by then a partner responsible for managing client relationships, led meetings with two key accounts. Afterward, the first client approached Snow and asked him to sit in on future meetings. Then the second client withdrew his business altogether, complaining that Geller had refused to listen to alternative points of view.

Contrast Geller's experience with that of 39-year-old Barry Kessler, a senior vice president at an insurance company. For years, Kessler had been heir apparent to the CEO due to his strong financial skills and vast knowledge of the business—that is, until John Mason, his boss and the current CEO, began to question the wisdom of promoting him.

While Kessler managed his own group exceptionally well, he avoided collaboration with other units, which was particularly important as the company began looking for new growth opportunities, including potential alliances with other organizations. The problem wasn't that Kessler was hostile, it was that he was passively disengaged—a flaw that hadn't seemed as important when he was responsible only for his own group. In coaching Kessler, we learned that he was extremely averse to conflict and that he avoided situations where he couldn't be the decision maker. His aversions sharply limited his ability to work with peers.

Mason sent a strong signal, not only to Kessler but to others in the organization, when he essentially demoted Kessler by taking away some of his responsibilities and temporarily pulling him from the succession plan. To give Kessler an opportunity to develop the skills he lacked, Mason asked him to lead a cross-functional team dedicated to finding strategic opportunities for growth. Success would require Kessler to devote more time to developing his interpersonal skills. He had no authority over the other team members, so he had to work through disputes and help the team arrive at a consensus. Two years later, Kessler reports that he is more comfortable with conflict and feedback, and he's worked his way back into the succession plan.

By the way, it's counterproductive to hold managers to a certain standard of behavior without showing that the same standard applies to everyone, right up to top management. In many cases, that means acknowledging your own development goals, which isn't easy. One CEO we worked with, Joe Simons, came to realize during 360-degree feedback and peer coaching that his personal style was interfering with his subordinates' growth.

Simons had declared innovation a corporate priority, yet his fear of failure led him to micromanage his employees, stifling their creativity. To stop this pattern and express his newfound commitment to improving his relationship skills, he revealed his personal goals—to seek advice more regularly and to communicate more openly—to his direct reports. He promised to change specific behaviors and asked for the team's feedback and support in this process. Going public with these goals was tough for Simons, a private person raised on traditional command-and-control leadership. Admitting that he needed to change some behaviors felt dangerously weak to him, especially given that the company was going through a difficult time and employees were looking to him for assurance, but his actions made his new priorities clear to employees.

Simons's candor won people's trust and respect, and over the course of many months, others in the company began to reflect more openly on their own emotional skills and engage in similar processes of personal development. Not only did his relationships with his direct reports improve, but Simons became a catalyst and model for others as well. He told us of an encounter with Gwen Marshall, the company's CFO and one of Simons's direct reports. Marshall was concerned about a new hire who wasn't coming up to speed as quickly as she had hoped—he was asking lots of questions and, she felt, not taking enough initiative. She had just snapped at him at the close of a meeting, and he'd looked surprised and angry. In speaking to Simons about the incident, however, she acknowledged that her impatience was perhaps unfair. He was, after all, new to the job. What's more, the nature of finance demanded precise thinking and a thorough knowledge of the business. Marshall ended the conversation by saying she would apologize to the new employee. Simons was surprised at Marshall's comments—he was used to seeing her simply blow off steam and move on to the next task. But possibly due to Simons's example, she had become more attuned to the importance of her own emotional competence. Such reflection has become a habit among Simons's team—a change that has enhanced personal relationships and increased the team's overall performance.

INSTITUTIONALIZE PERSONAL DEVELOPMENT

One of the most effective ways to build managers' emotional competencies is to weave interpersonal goals into the fabric of the organization, where everyone is expected to demonstrate a specific set of emotional skills and where criteria for promotion include behaviors as well as technical ability. A built-in process will make it easier to uncover potential problems early and reduce the chances that people identified as needing personal development will feel singled out or unfairly held back. Employees will know exactly what's expected of them and what it takes to advance in their careers.

Here's a case in which institutionalizing personal development was extremely effective: Mark Jones is an executive who was tapped for the CEO job at a major manufacturing company on the condition that he engage a coach because of his reputation for being too blunt and aggressive. A yearlong coaching relationship helped Jones understand the pitfalls associated with his style, and he decided that others could benefit from arriving at such an understanding far earlier in their careers. To that end, he launched several major initiatives to shape the company culture in such a way that personal and professional learning were not only encouraged but expected.

First, he articulated a new set of corporate values and practices that were based on meeting business objectives and developing top-notch leadership skills. One of the values was "Dare to be transparent," which meant that all employees, especially those in senior leadership roles, were expected to be open about their weaknesses, ask for help, and offer honest, constructive feedback to their peers. Knowing that it would be necessary to create incentives and rewards for these new behaviors, Jones took an active role in the review and personal-development goals of the company's top 100 executives, and he mandated that all employees' performance plans incorporate specific actions related to developing their own emotional competencies. Jones also made emotional skills a key qualification in the search for a successor—a requirement that many organizations pay lip service to. Many of them often overvalue raw intellect and depth of knowledge, largely because of the war for talent, which has resulted in a singular focus on hiring and retaining the best and brightest regardless of their emotional competence. Finally, Jones created a new position, corporate learning officer; he and the CLO partnered with a nearby university to create a learning institute where corporate executives could teach in and attend leadership programs. Jones himself is a frequent lecturer and participant in the various courses.

Through all these actions, Jones has made it clear that employees need to make continual learning and emotional development a priority. He's also emphasized that everyone from the CEO on down is expected to set goals for improving personal skills. Since implementing the program, he is finding it easier to attract and retain talented young executives—indeed, his organization has evolved from a recruiter's nightmare to a magnet for young talent. It is becoming known as a place where emerging leaders can find real opportunities to learn and grow.

We worked with another company where the senior management team committed to developing the emotional competencies of the company's leaders. The team first provided extensive education on coaching to the HR department, which in turn supervised a program whereby top managers coached their younger and more inexperienced colleagues. The goal was to have both the experienced and inexperienced benefit: The junior managers provided feedback on the senior people's coaching skills, and the senior people helped foster emotional competencies in their less-experienced colleagues.

The results were encouraging. Wes Burke, an otherwise high-performing manager, had recently been struggling to meet his business targets. After spending time with Burke and conferring with his subordinates and peers, his coach (internal to the organization) came to believe that, in his zest to achieve his goals, Burke was unable to slow down and listen to other people's ideas. Burke wasn't a boor: He had taken courses in communication and knew how to fake listening behaviors such as nodding his head and giving verbal acknowledgments, but he was often distracted and not really paying attention. He never accepted this feedback until one day, while he was walking purposefully through the large operations plant he managed, a floor supervisor stopped him to discuss his ideas for solving an ongoing production problem. Burke flipped on his active-listening mode.

After uttering a few acknowledgments and saying, "Thanks, let's talk more about that," he moved on, leaving the supervisor feeling frustrated and at a loss for how to capture his boss's interest. As it happened, Burke's coach was watching. He pulled the young manager aside and said, "You didn't hear a word Karl just said. You weren't really listening." Burke admitted as much to himself and his coach. He then apologized to Karl, much to the supervisor's surprise. Keeping this incident in mind helped Burke remember the importance of his working relationships. His coach had also helped him realize that he shouldn't have assumed his sheer will and drive would somehow motivate his employees. Burke had been wearing people down, physically and psychologically. A year later, Burke's operation was hitting its targets, an accomplishment he partially attributes to the one-on-one coaching he received.

CULTIVATE INFORMAL NETWORKS

While institutionalized programs to build emotional competencies are critical, some managers will benefit more from an informal network of relationships that fall outside the company hierarchy. Mentoring, for example, can help both junior and senior managers further their emotional development through a new type of relationship. And when the mentoring experience is a positive one, it often acts as a springboard to a rich variety of relationships with others throughout the organization. In particular, it gives junior managers a chance to experience different leadership styles and exposes them to diverse viewpoints.

Sonia Greene, a 32-year-old manager at a consulting firm, was hoping to be promoted to principal, but she hadn't raised the issue with her boss because she assumed he didn't think she was ready, and she didn't want to create tension. She was a talented consultant with strong client relationships, but her internal relationships were weak due to a combination of shyness, an independent nature, and a distaste for conflict, which inhibited her from asking for feedback. When her company launched a mentoring program, Greene signed up, and through a series of lengthy conversations with Jessica Burnham, a partner at the firm, she developed new insights about her strengths and weaknesses. The support of an established player such as Burnham helped Greene become more confident and honest in her development discussions with her boss, who hadn't been aware that Greene was willing to receive and act on feedback. Today, Greene is armed with a precise understanding of what she needs to work on and is well on her way to being promoted. What's more, her relationship with Burnham has prompted her to seek out other connections, including a peer group of up-and-coming managers who meet monthly to share experiences and offer advice to one another.

Peer networking is beneficial to even the most top-level executives. And the relationships needn't be confined within organizational boundaries. Joe Simons, a CEO we mentioned earlier, wanted to continue his own personal development, so he cultivated a relationship with another executive he'd met through our program. The two men have stayed in touch through regular e-mails and phone calls, keeping their discussions confidential so they can feel free to share even the most private concerns. They also get together periodically to discuss their goals for personal development. Both have found these meetings invaluable, noting that their work relationships have continued to improve and that having a trustworthy confidant has helped each avoid relapsing into old habits during times of stress.

Delaying a promotion can be difficult given the steadfast ambitions of the young executive and the hectic pace of organizational life, which makes personal learning seem like an extravagance. It requires a delicate balance of honesty and support, of patience and goading. It means going against the norm of promoting people almost exclusively on smarts, talent, and business results. It also means contending with the disappointment of an esteemed subordinate.

But taking the time to build people's emotional competencies isn't an extravagance; it's critical to developing effective leaders. Give in to the temptation to promote your finest before they're ready, and you're left with executives who may thrive on change and demonstrate excellent coping and survival skills but who lack the self-awareness, empathy, and social abilities required to foster and nurture those strengths in others. MBA programs and management books can't teach young executives everything they need to know about people skills. Indeed, there's no substitute for experience, reflection, feedback, and, above all, practice.

Think Before Promoting

IT'S NOT UNUSUAL FOR a star performer to be promoted into higher management before he's ready. Yes, he may be exceptionally smart and talented, but he may also lack essential people skills. Rather than denying him the promotion altogether, his boss might do well to delay it—and use that time to help develop the candidate's emotional competencies. Here's how.

Deepen 360-Degree Feedback

Go beyond the usual set of questionnaires that make up the traditional 360-degree-feedback process. Interview a wide variety of the manager's peers and subordinates and let him read verbatim responses to open-ended performance questions.

Interrupt the Ascent

Help the inexperienced manager get beyond a command-and-control mentality by pushing him to develop his negotiation and persuasion skills. Instead of promoting him, give him cross-functional assignments where he can't rely on rank to influence people.

Act On Your Commitment

Don't give the inexperienced manager the impression that emotional competencies are optional. Hold him accountable for his interpersonal skills, in some cases taking a tough stance by demoting him or denying him a promotion, but with the promise that changed behaviors will ultimately be rewarded.

Institutionalize Personal Development

Weave interpersonal goals into the fabric of the organization and make emotional competence a performance measure. Also work to institute formal development programs that teach leadership skills and facilitate self-awareness, reflection, and opportunities to practice new emotional competencies.

Cultivate Informal Networks

Encourage the manager to develop informal learning partnerships with peers and mentors in order to expose him to different leadership styles and perspectives. This will provide him with honest and ongoing feedback and continual opportunities to learn.

Notes

1. In his HBR articles "What Makes a Leader?" (November–December 1998) and "Primal Leadership: The Hidden Driver of Great Performance" (with Richard Boyatzis and Annie McKee, December 2001), Daniel Goleman makes the case that emotional competence is the crucial driver of a leader's success.

Originally published in December 2002
Reprint R0212F

Saving Your Rookie Managers from Themselves

CAROL A. WALKER

Executive Summary

MOST ORGANIZATIONS PROMOTE employees into managerial positions based on their technical competence. But very often, that kind of competence does not translate into good managerial performance. Many rookie managers fail to grasp how their roles have changed: that their jobs are no longer about personal achievement but about enabling others to achieve, that sometimes driving the bus means taking a backseat, and that building a team is often more important than cutting a deal. Even the best employees have trouble adjusting to these new realities, and that trouble can be exacerbated by the normal insecurities that may make rookie managers hesitant to ask for help.

The dynamic unfolds something like this: As rookie managers internalize their stress, their focus, too, becomes increasingly internal. They become insecure and self-focused and cannot properly support their teams. Invariably, trust breaks down, staff members become alienated, and productivity suffers.

In this article, coach and management consultant Carol Walker, who works primarily with rookie managers and their supervisors, addresses the five problem areas that rookie managers typically face: delegating, getting support from senior staffers, projecting confidence, thinking strategically, and giving feedback. You may think these elements sound like Management 101, and you'd be right, Walker writes. But these basic elements are also what trip up most managers in the early stages of their careers (and even, she admits, throughout their careers). The bosses of rookie managers have a responsibility to anticipate and address these problems; not doing so will hurt the rookie, the boss, and the company overall.

T OM EDELMAN, LIKE A MILLION freshly minted managers before him, had done a marvelous job as an individual contributor. He was smart, confident, forward thinking, and resourceful. His clients liked him, as did his boss and coworkers. Consequently, no one in the department was surprised when his boss offered him a managerial position. Tom accepted with some ambivalence—he loved working directly with clients and was loath to give that up—but on balance, he was thrilled.

Six months later, when I was called in to coach Tom (I've disguised his name), I had trouble even picturing the confident insider he once had been. He looked like a deer caught in the headlights. Tom seemed overwhelmed and indeed even used that word several times to describe how he felt. He had started to doubt his abilities. His direct reports, once close colleagues, no longer seemed to respect or even like him. What's more, his department had been beset by a series of small crises, and Tom spent most of his time putting out these fires. He knew this wasn't the most effective use of his time, but he didn't know how to stop. These problems hadn't yet translated into poor business results, but he was in trouble nonetheless.

His boss realized that he was in danger of failing and brought me in to assist. With support and coaching, Tom got the help he needed and eventually became an effective manager. Indeed, he has been promoted twice since I worked with him, and he now runs a small division within the same company. But his near failure—and the path that brought him to that point—is surprisingly typical. Most organizations promote employees into managerial positions based on their technical competence. Very often, however, those people fail to grasp how their roles have changed—that their jobs are no longer about personal achievement but instead about enabling others to achieve, that sometimes driving the bus means taking a backseat, and that building a team is often more important than cutting a deal. Even the best employees can have trouble adjusting to these new realities. That trouble may be exacerbated by normal insecurities that make rookie managers hesitant to ask for help, even when they find themselves in thoroughly unfamiliar territory. As these new managers internalize their stress, their focus becomes internal as well. They become insecure and self-focused and cannot properly support their teams. Inevitably, trust breaks down, staff members are alienated, and productivity suffers.

Many companies unwittingly support this downward spiral by assuming that their rookie managers will somehow learn critical management skills by osmosis. Some rookies do, to be sure, but in my experience they're the exceptions. Most need more help. In the absence of comprehensive training and intensive coaching—which most companies don't offer—the rookie manager's boss plays a key role. Of course, it's not possible for most senior managers to spend hours and hours every week overseeing a new manager's work, but if you know what typical challenges a rookie manager faces, you'll be able to anticipate some problems before they arise and nip others in the bud.

Delegating

Effective delegation may be one of the most difficult tasks for rookie managers. Senior managers bestow on them big responsibilities and tight deadlines, and they put a lot of pressure on them to produce results. The natural response of rookies when faced with such challenges is to "just do it," thinking that's what got them promoted in the first place. But their reluctance to delegate assignments also has its roots in some very real fears. First is the fear of losing stature: If I assign high-profile projects to my staff members, they'll get the credit. What kind of visibility will I be left with? Will it be clear to my boss and my staff what value I'm adding? Second is the fear of abdicating control: If I allow Frank to do this, how can I be sure that he will do it correctly? In the face of this fear, the rookie manager may delegate tasks but supervise Frank so closely that he will never feel accountable. Finally, the rookie may be hesitant to delegate work because he's afraid of overburdening his staff. He may be uncomfortable assigning work to former peers for fear that they'll resent him. But the real resentment usually comes when staff members feel that lack of opportunity is blocking their advancement.

Signs that these fears may be playing out include new managers who work excessively long hours, are hesitant to take on new responsibilities, have staff members who seem unengaged, or have a tendency to answer on behalf of employees instead of encouraging them to communicate with you directly.

The first step toward helping young managers delegate effectively is to get them to understand their new role. Acknowledge that their job fundamentally differs from an individual contributor's. Clarify what you and the organization value in leaders. Developing talented, promotable staff is critical in any company. Let new managers know that they will be rewarded for these less tangible efforts in addition to hitting numerical goals. Understanding this new role is half the battle for rookie managers, and one that many companies mistakenly assume is evident from the start.

After clarifying how your rookie manager's role has changed, you can move on to tactics. Perhaps it goes without saying, but you should lead by example. You have the responsibility to empower the rookie who works for you and do what you can to help him overcome his insecurities about his value to the organization. You can then assist him in looking for opportunities to empower and engage his team.

One young manager I worked with desperately needed to find time to train and supervise new employees. His firm had been recently acquired, and he had to deal with high staff turnover and new industry wide rules and regulations. The most senior person on his staff—a woman who had worked for the acquiring company—was about to return from an extended family leave, and he was convinced that he couldn't ask her for help. After all, she had a part-time schedule, and she'd asked to be assigned to the company's largest client. To complicate matters, he suspected that she resented his promotion. As we evaluated the situation, the manager was able to see that the senior staffer's number one priority was reestablishing herself as an important part of the team. Once he realized this, he asked her to take on critical supervisory responsibilities, balanced with a smaller client load, and she eagerly agreed. Indeed, she returned from leave excited about partnering with her manager to develop the team.

When a new manager grumbles about mounting workloads, seize the opportunity to discuss delegation. Encourage him to take small risks initially, playing to the obvious strengths of his staff members. Asking his super-organized, reliable assistant to take the lead in handling the logistics of a new product launch, for example, is much less risky than asking a star salesperson, unaccustomed to this sort of detailed work, to do it. Early successes will build the manager's confidence and willingness to take progressively larger risks in stretching each team member's capabilities. Reinforce to him that delegation does not mean abdication. Breaking a complex project into manageable chunks, each with clearly defined milestones, makes effective follow-up easier. It's also important to schedule regular meetings before the project even begins in order to ensure that the manager stays abreast of progress and that staff members feel accountable.

Getting Support from Above

Most first-time managers see their relationship with their boss more as one of servitude than of partnership. They will wait for you to initiate meetings, ask for reports, and question results. You may welcome this restraint, but generally it's a bad sign. For one thing, it puts undue pressure on you to keep the flow of communication going. Even more important, it prevents new managers from looking to you as a critical source of support. If they don't see you that way, it's unlikely that they will see themselves that way for their own people. The problem isn't only that your position intimidates them; it's also that they fear being vulnerable. A newly promoted manager doesn't want you to see weaknesses, lest you think you made a mistake in promoting her. When I ask rookie managers about their relationships with their bosses, they often admit that they are trying to "stay under the boss's radar" and are "careful about what [they] say to the boss."

Some inexperienced managers will not seek your help even when they start to founder. Seemingly capable rookie managers often try to cover up a failing project or relationship—just until they can get it back under control. For example, one manager I worked with at a technology company hired a professional 20 years her senior. The transition was rocky, and, despite her best efforts, the individual wasn't acclimating to the organization. (The company, like many in the technology sector, was very youth oriented.) Rather than reaching out to her boss for help, the manager continued to grapple with the situation alone. The staff member ultimately resigned at the busiest time of the year, and the young manager suffered the dual punishment of being understaffed at the worst possible moment and having it known that she had lost a potentially important contributor.

What's the boss of a rookie manager to do? You can begin by clarifying expectations. Explain the connection between the rookie's success and your success, so that she understands that open communication is necessary for you to achieve your goals. Explain that you don't expect her to have all the answers. Introduce her to other managers within the company who may be helpful, and encourage her to contact them as needed. Let her know that mistakes happen but that the cover-up is always worse than the crime. Let her know that you like to receive occasional lunch invitations as much as you like to extend them.

Lunch and drop-by meetings are important, but they usually aren't enough. Consider meeting regularly with a new manager—perhaps weekly in the early stages of a new assignment, moving to biweekly or monthly as her confidence builds. These meetings will develop rapport, provide you with insight into how the person is approaching the job, and make the new manager organize her thoughts on a regular basis. Be clear that the meetings are her time and that it's up to her to plan the agenda. You're there to ask and answer questions and to offer advice. The message you send is that the individual's work is important to you and that you're a committed business partner. More subtly, you're modeling how to simultaneously empower and guide direct reports.

Projecting Confidence

Looking confident when you don't feel confident—it's a challenge we all face, and as senior managers we're usually conscious of the need when it arises. Rookie managers are often so internally focused that they are unaware of this need or the image they project. They are so focused on substance that they forget that form counts, too. The first weeks and months on the job are a critical time for new leaders to reach out to staff. If they don't project confidence, they are unlikely to inspire and energize their teams.

I routinely work with new managers who are unaware that their everyday demeanor is hurting their organizations. In one rapidly growing technology company, the service manager, Linda, faced high levels of stress. Service outages were all too common, and they were beyond her control. Customers were exacting, and they too were under great pressure. Her rapidly growing staff was generally inexperienced. Distraught customers and employees had her tied up in knots almost daily. She consistently appeared breathless, rushed, and fearful that the other shoe was about to drop. The challenge was perhaps too big for a first-time manager, but that's what happens in rapidly growing companies. On one level, Linda was doing an excellent job keeping the operation going. The client base was growing and retention was certainly high—largely as a result of her energy and resourcefulness. But on another level, she was doing a lot of damage.

Linda's frantic demeanor had two critical repercussions. First, she had unwittingly defined the standard for acceptable conduct in her department, and her inexperienced staff began to display the same behaviors. Before long, other departments were reluctant to communicate with Linda or her team, for fear of bothering them or eliciting an emotional reaction. But for the company to arrive at real solutions to the service problems, departments needed to openly exchange information, and that wasn't happening. Second, Linda was not portraying herself to senior managers as promotion material. They were pleased with her troubleshooting abilities, but they did not see a confident, thoughtful senior manager in the making. The image Linda was projecting would ultimately hold back both her career and her department.

Not all rookie managers display the problems that Linda did. Some appear excessively arrogant. Others wear their self-doubt on their sleeves. Whether your managers appear overwhelmed, arrogant, or insecure, honest feedback is your best tool. You can help rookie managers by telling them that it's always safe to let out their feelings—in your office, behind closed doors. Reinforce just how long a shadow they cast once they assume leadership positions. Their staff members watch them closely, and if they see professionalism and optimism, they are likely to demonstrate those characteristics as well. Preach the gospel of conscious comportment—a constant awareness of the image one is projecting to the world. If you observe a manager projecting a less-than-positive image, tell that person right away.

You should also be alert to new managers who undermine their own authority. Linda made another classic rookie mistake when she attempted to get her staff members to implement an initiative that her boss had come up with. In presenting the initiative, she let her team know it was important to implement because it had come from the division's senior vice president. While her intentions were good—rallying the team to perform—her words encouraged the group to focus attention above her rather than on her. There is no quicker way for a rookie manager to lose credibility with her staff than to appear to be a mouthpiece for senior management. Pointing out that senior management will be checking up on the initiative certainly won't hurt, but the rookie manager must take care never to be perceived simply as the messenger.

Just-in-time coaching is often the most effective method for showing rookie managers how to project confidence. For instance, the first time you ask a new manager to carry out an initiative, take a little extra time to walk her through the process. Impress upon her the cardinal rule of management: Your staff members don't necessarily have to like you, but they do need to trust you. Ensure that the new manager owns the message she's delivering.

Layoffs are a classic example of a message the rookie manager will struggle with. Don't allow a rookie to proceed half-prepared. Share as much information as you can. Make sure she's ready for all the likely questions and reactions by asking her to do an informal dry run with you. You might be surprised by how poorly she conveys the message in her first few attempts. A little practice may preserve the image of your manager and your company.

Focusing on the Big Picture

Rookie managers have a real knack for allowing immediate tasks to overshadow overarching initiatives. This is particularly true for those promoted from within, because they've just come from the front lines where they're accustomed to constant fire fighting. As a recent individual contributor armed with plenty of technical know-how, the rookie manager instinctively runs to the immediate rescue of any client or staff member in need. The sense of accomplishment rookies get from such rescues is seductive and far more exhilarating than rooting out the cause of all the fire fighting. And what could be better for team spirit than having the boss jump into the trenches and fight the good fight?

Of course, a leader shows great team spirit if he joins the troops in emergencies. But are all those emergencies true emergencies? Are newer staff members being empowered to handle complex challenges? And if the rookie manager is busy fighting fires, who is thinking strategically for the department? If you're the senior manager and these questions are popping into your head, you may well have a rookie manager who doesn't fully understand his role or is afraid to seize it.

I recently worked with a young manager who had become so accustomed to responding to a steady flow of problems that he was reluctant to block off any time to work on the strategic initiatives we had identified. When I probed, he revealed that he felt a critical part of his role was to wait for crises to arise. "What if I schedule this time and something urgent comes up and I disappoint someone?" he asked. When I pointed out that he could always postpone his strategy sessions if a true emergency arose, he seemed relieved. But he saw the concept of making time to think about the business as self-indulgent—this, despite the fact that his group was going to be asked to raise productivity significantly in the following fiscal year, and he'd done nothing to prepare for that reality.

Senior managers can help rookies by explaining to them that strategic thinking is a necessary skill for career advancement: For first-time managers, 10% of the work might be strategic and 90% tactical. As executives climb the corporate ladder, however, those percentages will flip-flop. To be successful at the next level, managers must demonstrate that they can think and act strategically. You can use your regularly scheduled meetings to help your managers focus on the big picture. Don't allow them to simply review the latest results and move on. Ask probing questions about those results. For example, "What trends are you seeing in the marketplace that could affect you in two quarters? Tell me how your competition is responding to those same trends." Don't let them regale you with the wonderful training their staffs have been getting without asking, "What additional skills do we need to build in the staff to increase productivity by 25% next year?" If you aren't satisfied with your managers' responses, let them know that you expect them to think this way—not to have all the answers, but to be fully engaged in the strategic thought process.

Rookie managers commonly focus on activities rather than on goals. That's because activities can be accomplished quickly (for example, conducting a seminar to improve the sales staff's presentation skills), whereas achieving goals generally takes more time (for example, actually enhancing the sales staff's effectiveness). The senior manager can help the rookie manager think strategically by asking for written goals that clearly distinguish between the goals and their supporting activities. Insisting on a goal-setting discipline will help your new (and not-so-new) managers to organize their strategic game plans. Critical but soft goals, such as staff development, are often overlooked because they are difficult to measure. Putting such goals in print with clear action steps makes them concrete, rendering a sense of accomplishment when they are achieved and a greater likelihood that they will be rewarded. Managers with clear goals will be less tempted to become full-time tacticians.

Just as important, the process will help you ensure that they are thinking about the right issues and deploying their teams effectively.

Giving Constructive Feedback

It's human nature to avoid confrontations, and most people feel awkward when they have to correct others' behavior or actions. Rookie managers are no exception, and they often avoid addressing important issues with their staff. The typical scenario goes something like this: A staff member is struggling to meet performance goals or is acting inappropriately in meetings. The manager sits back, watches, and hopes that things will magically improve. Other staff members observe the situation and become frustrated by the manager's inaction. The manager's own frustration builds, as she can't believe the subordinate doesn't get it. The straight-forward performance issue has now evolved into a credibility problem. When the manager finally addresses the problem, she personalizes it, lets her frustration seep into the discussion with her staff member, and finds the recipient rushing to defend himself from attack.

Most inexperienced managers wait far too long to talk with staff about performance problems. The senior manager can help by creating an environment in which constructive feedback is perceived not as criticism but as a source of empowerment. This begins with the feedback you offer to your managers about their own development. It can be as simple as getting them to tell you where their weaknesses are before they become problematic. After a good performance review, for example, you might say to your new manager, "By all accounts, you have a bright future here, so it's important that we talk about what you *don't* want me to know. What are you feeling least confident about? How can we address those areas so that you're ready for any opportunity that arises?" You'll probably be surprised by how attuned most high performers are to their own development needs. But they are not likely to do much about them unless you put those needs on the table.

More than likely, the feedback your managers have to offer their staffs will not always be so positive or easy to deliver. The key is to foster in them the desire to help their reports achieve their goals. Under those circumstances, even loathsome personal issues become approachable.

One of my clients managed a high-performing senior staff member who was notably unhelpful to others in the department and who resented her own lack of advancement. Instead of avoiding the issue because he didn't want to tell the staff member that she had a bad attitude, the senior manager took a more productive approach. He leveraged his knowledge of her personal goals to introduce the feedback. "I know that you're anxious for your first management role, and one of my goals is to help you attain that. I can't do that unless I'm completely honest with you. A big part of management is developing stronger skills in your staff. You aren't demonstrating that you enjoy that role. How can we can work together on that?" No guilt, no admonishment—just an offer to help her get what she wanted. Yet the message was received loud and clear.

A brainstorming session this client and I had about ways to offer critical feedback led to that approach. Often, brainstorming sessions can help rookie managers see that sticky personal issues can be broken down into straightforward business issues. In the case of the unhelpful senior staff member, her attitude didn't really need to enter the discussion; her actions did. Recommending a change in action is much easier than recommending a change in attitude. Never forget the old saw: You can't ask people to change their personalities, but you can ask them to change their behaviors.

Indeed, senior managers should share their own techniques for dealing with difficult conversations. One manager I worked with became defensive whenever a staff member questioned her judgment. She didn't really need me to tell her that her behavior was undermining her image and effectiveness. She did need me to offer her some techniques that would enable her to respond differently in the heat of the moment. She trained herself to respond quickly and earnestly with a small repertoire of questions like, "Can you tell me more about what you mean by that?" This simple technique bought her the time she needed to gather her thoughts and engage in an interchange that was productive rather than defensive. She was too close to the situation to come up with the technique herself.

D ELEGATING, thinking strategically, communicating—you may think this all sounds like Management 101. And you're right. The most basic elements of management are often what trip up managers early in their careers. And because they are the basics, the bosses of rookie managers often take them for granted. They shouldn't—an extraordinary number of people fail to develop these skills. I've maintained an illusion throughout this article—that only rookie managers suffer because they haven't mastered these core skills. But the truth is, managers at all levels make these mistakes. An organization that supports its new managers by helping them to develop these skills will have surprising advantages over the competition.

Originally published in April 2002
Reprint R0204H

About the Contributors

BETH AXELROD is a Principal at McKinsey & Company in Stamford, Connecticut.

KERRY A. BUNKER is a Manager of the Awareness Program for Executive Excellence at the Center for Creative Leadership in Greensboro, North Carolina.

TIMOTHY BUTLER is a Research Fellow and the Director of career development programs at Harvard Business School.

HELEN HANDFIELD-JONES is a Senior Practice Expert at McKinsey & Company in Toronto.

JAY M. JACKMAN is a psychiatrist and human resources consultant in Stanford, California.

ELLIOTT JAQUES was one of the world's leading psychologists and a pioneer in human development theory.

KATHY E. KRAM is a professor of organizational behavior at the Boston University School of Management.

HARRY LEVINSON is Chairman of The Levinson Institute and Clinical Professor of Psychology Emeritus in the Department of Psychiatry, Harvard Medical School.

ED MICHAELS is a retired Director of McKinsey & Company in Atlanta.

MAURY A. PEIPERL is Associate Dean and Director of the Careers Research Initiative at London Business School, and a Director of Learning Designs Limited, a management consulting firm.

MYRA H. STROBER is a labor economist and professor at Stanford University's School of Education, and by courtesy at the Stanford Graduate School of Business. She is also a human resources consultant.

SHARON TING is a Manager of the Awareness Program for Executive Excellence at the Center for Creative Leadership in Greensboro, North Carolina.

JAMES WALDROOP is a Founding Principal of Peregrine Partners, a consulting firm in Brookline, Massachusetts, that specializes in executive development and employee retention.

CAROL A. WALKER is the President of Prepared to Lead, a management consulting firm in Weston, Massachusetts. Before founding the company, she worked for 15 years as an executive in the insurance and technology industries.

Index